Annual Survey 2006

US Government & Politics

Anthony J. Bennett

[redacted]

Philip Allan Updates
Market Place
Deddington
Oxfordshire
OX15 0SE

tel: 01869 338652
fax: 01869 337590
e-mail: sales@philipallan.co.uk
www.philipallan.co.uk

ISBN-10: 1-88489-422-3
ISBN-13: 978-1-84489-422-2

Printed by Raithby, Lawrence & Co Ltd, Leicester

Environmental information
The paper on which this title is printed is sourced from managed, sustainable forests.

P00610

Contents

Preface

With the re-election of President George W. Bush, 2004 was a year of continuation. With two vacancies in the nine-member Supreme Court, 2005 was a year of change. The resignation of Sandra Day O'Connor, followed closely by the death of William Rehnquist, gave President Bush two opportunities to change the shape of the Supreme Court. In this year's edition, we analyse the nomination of John Roberts to replace William Rehnquist as chief justice of the United States. But the vacancy brought about by the retirement of Sandra Day O'Connor has taken much longer to fill. Indeed, between July and November, three different people were nominated by the President to fill this vacancy — John Roberts, Harriet Miers and Samuel Alito. The Roberts nomination was withdrawn so that the President could nominate him for the post of chief justice. Then Miers withdrew, leaving Alito as the likely replacement. We shall consider this story in the 2007 edition.

Elsewhere we review the Bush Cabinet as well as assessing the legacy of Bush's first term. It is something of a paradox that although re-election seems to be a necessary ingredient for a 'great' presidency, second terms in themselves have often courted disaster — think Johnson and Vietnam, Nixon and Watergate, Reagan and Iran–Contra or Clinton and impeachment. One of the problems that modern-day presidents face throughout their second terms is the status of lame duck, following the passage of the 22nd Amendment (1951), which forbids even the possibility of a third term. It is this unintended consequence of the presidential term limit that makes me seriously question its wisdom.

One of only 11 US presidents to serve two full terms in office was Ronald Reagan. This year (2006) marks the 25th anniversary of the coming to office of this popular but controversial president. In this edition we assess Reagan's legacy. How did someone who once starred in a film with a chimpanzee end up as president of the United States, and then go on to receive the accolade of being 'a very great political leader' from Soviet president Mikhail Gorbachev?

The mid-term elections will take place on Tuesday 7 November 2006. Democrats have high hopes that 12 years of Republican control of Congress, plus Republican scandals — mainly those surrounding Lewis (Scooter) Libby, the former chief of staff to Vice President Cheney, and Tom DeLay, the former House Majority Leader — will swing enough races in their direction to allow them a real shot at retaking control of both houses of Congress. But some commentators are less sure. What we do know for certain is that as soon as those elections are over, the starting gun for the 2008 presidential race will sound. Who to watch? Will Hillary Clinton run for the Democrats? What about John McCain or George Allen on the Republican side? Time will tell.

Anthony J. Bennett
Charterhouse, Godalming, Surrey

Chapter 1

The Bush cabinet

What you need to know

- The president's cabinet is an advisory group selected by the president to aid him in making decisions.
- It is not mentioned in the Constitution.
- All the heads of the 15 executive departments are ex officio members of the cabinet.
- Nominations are made by the president.
- The Senate has the power to give 'advice and consent' on these nominations.
- The president may award cabinet rank to other executive branch officials at his discretion.
- Cabinet meetings can serve a number of useful functions.
- Cabinet meetings usually decline in frequency during an administration.
- Under many presidents, cabinet meetings came to be regarded as a waste of time.

First-term turnover

By the end of President George W. Bush's first term, 12 of the original 14 cabinet officers were still at their posts. Only Treasury Secretary Paul O'Neill and Housing and Urban Development (HUD) Secretary Mel Martinez had left the cabinet during Bush's first 4 years. Their respective replacements were John Snow and Alphonso Jackson. Tom Ridge had also joined the Bush cabinet in 2003 as Secretary of the newly created Department of Homeland Security.

All this made the George W. Bush cabinet the most stable of first-term cabinets in modern times. With only two departures, Bush's first term easily outclassed those of Richard Nixon, Jimmy Carter, Ronald Reagan, George Bush and Bill Clinton, as is shown in Table 1.1.

President	Dates of first term	Number of cabinet replacement appointments
Richard Nixon	1969–73	8
Jimmy Carter	1977–81	8
Ronald Reagan	1981–85	5
George Bush	1989–93	8
Bill Clinton	1993–97	4
George W. Bush	2001–05	2

***Table 1.1** Number of cabinet replacement appointments during presidents' first terms since 1969*

Second-term changes

But if George W. Bush's first term was noteworthy for its cabinet stability, the start of the second term was remarkable for quite the opposite reason. Between election day (2 November 2004) and Inauguration Day (20 January 2005), 9 of the 15 cabinet officers were shown the door. Admittedly, most presidents use the start of a second term for some political spring-cleaning. Reagan got rid of 7 cabinet officers before the start of his second term, while Clinton made 8 changes before the start of his. George W. Bush made 9 changes, just short of the 10 made by Nixon in January 1973. The exits and entrances of the Bush cabinet that occurred during these 10 weeks are shown in Table 1.2.

Department	Departing	Replaced by
State	Colin Powell	Condoleezza Rice
Justice (Attorney General)	John Ashcroft	Alberto Gonzales
Agriculture	Ann Veneman	Michael Johanns
Commerce	Don Evans	Carlos Gutierrez
Health and Human Services	Tommy Thompson	Michael Leavitt
Energy	Spencer Abraham	Samuel Bodman
Education	Rod Paige	Margaret Spellings
Veterans' Affairs	Anthony Principi	Jim Nicholson
Homeland Security	Tom Ridge	Michael Chertoff

Table 1.2 Cabinet changes by George W. Bush, November 2004–January 2005

In the switch of Condoleezza Rice for Colin Powell at the State Department, President Bush set up the possibility that not only will he go down in history as the first president to appoint an African-American to this top cabinet post, but that African-Americans will head the State Department throughout his entire presidency. Dr Rice becomes the first black woman to hold the post. At just 51 years of age, she has already been a Special Assistant for Soviet and East European Affairs to the first George Bush (1989–91), served 6 years as Provost of Stanford University (1993–99), and then for 4 years was National Security Advisor (2001–05). She is also an accomplished concert pianist.

Another person moving from the White House to a downtown executive department was Alberto Gonzales, who had spent the first term as White House Counsel. Many were hoping that Gonzales would bring a less abrasive style and a less ideological perspective to the role of Attorney General — head of the Justice Department — than did his immediate predecessor, John Ashcroft. Gonzales, who comes from Texas, has sometimes been mentioned as a possible US Supreme Court pick if Bush has further vacancies to fill later in his second term. Both Rice and Gonzales are excellent examples of the policy specialists so often chosen by presidents to head up cabinet departments.

And so is the new Agriculture Secretary, Mike Johanns. Born in Iowa, he grew up doing chores on the family dairy farm. He still describes himself as 'a farmer's son with an intense passion for agriculture'. Neither is Johanns new to politics, having served 8 years as Mayor of Lincoln, Nebraska, before being elected state governor in 1998.

Carlos Gutierrez, the new Commerce Secretary, adds further to the ethnic diversity of the Bush cabinet. Born in Havana, Cuba, in 1953, he came to the United States with his family in 1960. Having started as a street salesman in Miami, he rose to become the youngest chief executive officer of Kellogg's in its 100-year history, eventually being appointed chairman of the board in 2000. That's not a bad example of both 'the American Dream' and 'the land of opportunity'. In explaining why he was nominating Gutierrez, President Bush stated that it was because the new Commerce Secretary 'understands the world of business, from the first rung on the ladder to the very top'.

Another former state governor — this time from Utah — is Mike Leavitt, the new Secretary of Health and Human Services. He became the nation's longest-serving governor during his 11-year tenure before moving to Washington in Bush's first term as Administrator of the Environmental Protection Agency (EPA). In 1994, the Utah state legislature passed into law Governor Leavitt's 'healthprint', a comprehensive, incremental healthcare policy for the state — at just the same time as President Clinton's national healthcare reforms were grinding to a halt in Congress. A decade later, Utah has nearly half-a-million more people with health insurance but a cost of healthcare per capita that is 25% below the national average. It sounds like he knows about healthcare policy.

The new Energy Secretary, Samuel Bodman, is now working in his third executive department in Washington, having previously been number two at both Commerce (2001–04) and the Treasury (2004–05). A financier by profession, Bodman brings no experience in energy-related issues. And at 67, he doesn't do much for the cabinet's average age.

Quite the opposite is the case with Margaret Spellings who replaces Rod Paige at Education. The 48-year-old mother of two spent the first term in the White House serving as a domestic policy advisor on education, and was one of those who crafted the No Child Left Behind Act, President Bush's signature education reform. Like her predecessor, she previously held education-related posts in Texas, where she was Director of the Texas Association of School Boards — yet another policy specialist.

The new Veterans' Affairs Secretary, Jim Nicholson, is best remembered in Washington for his time as chairman of the Republican National Committee between 1997 and 2001. Nicholson was therefore partly credited with the winning of the 2000 election. For the 4 years of Bush's first term, Nicholson served as US Ambassador to the Vatican. His military credentials include his graduation from West Point Military Academy in 1961 and his service in Vietnam, where he won numerous gallantry awards.

The final cabinet vacancy went — eventually — to Michael Chertoff as Secretary of Homeland Security. But that was after the only hiccup in the Bush cabinet replacement story — the withdrawal of Bernard Kerik. Kerik was a high-profile, some might say heroic, character who at the time of 9/11 was the New York City Police Commissioner. He withdrew from consideration for the post after revelations that he had employed an illegal immigrant as a housekeeper and nanny. The 'safe' and much more low-key replacement was Judge Michael Chertoff, a former US Appeals Court judge.

Senate confirmation

All these new cabinet members were, of course, subject to Senate confirmation. This is a two-stage process which begins in the relevant Senate standing committee before moving to the Senate chamber. Most of these nominations proved to be uncontroversial. They sailed through the committee hearings and were often approved by a **voice vote** on the Senate floor. Six of the nine new cabinet members were approved by voice vote, and a seventh — Homeland Security Secretary, Michael Chertoff — received a unanimous (98–0) recorded vote on the Senate floor. The only two to engender any degree of controversy were Secretary of State Condoleezza Rice and Attorney General Alberto Gonzales.

> **Key word**
>
> **voice vote:** a vote in a legislative chamber by which the presiding officer asks all those in favour of a proposal to say 'aye' and then asks all those opposed to say 'no'. He then determines which side has the largest support and declares that side to be the winner. There is therefore no record of how individual members have voted.

The Senate scheduled a 9-hour debate on the Condoleezza Rice nomination. Democrats tried rather lamely to make something out of very little in an effort to add significance to their advice and consent powers, as granted by Article II of the Constitution. But at the end of the debate, Rice was confirmed easily by 85 votes to 13.

The 'no' votes were made up of liberal Democrats such as Barbara Boxer (California), John Kerry (Massachusetts), Tom Harkin (Iowa) and Ted Kennedy (Massachusetts), who used the vote to show their disenchantment with the situation in Iraq. These Democrats were critical of Rice's role — while National Security Advisor in the first term — in arguing that Saddam Hussein had weapons of mass destruction.

But Republicans criticised some Democrat senators — notably Barbara Boxer of California — for politicising the confirmation hearings. Boxer had issued a fundraising letter for the Democratic Senatorial Campaign Committee that claimed that Republicans 'didn't count on me to ask the tough questions' about Condoleezza Rice. Rice spokesman Jim Wilkinson said the letter 'puts to rest any doubts some may have had that this is all about politics'.

'The speechmakers' zeal only delays the inevitable'

by Dana Milbank

Oh, the suspense! Two hours into the 9-hour Senate debate yesterday over Condoleezza Rice, Richard J. Durbin (Illinois), the Number 2 Democrat in the Senate, was asked whether he would vote to confirm. 'I'll be making a statement,' he said coyly.

Senator Robert Byrd (Democrat–West Virginia), a master of eighteenth-century and nineteenth-century rhetoric, strode onto the Senate floor carrying the text of an hour-long speech. 'In Federalist Number 77,' the 87-year-old lawmaker began, producing groans in the press gallery. Democrats, furious that White House Chief of Staff Andrew Card had said that their insistence on a full day of debate [on the Rice nomination] was 'petty politics', were determined to show that they were fulfilling their constitutional obligations. 'I am particularly dismayed by accusations I have read that Senate Democrats have somehow been engaged in nothing more substantial than petty politics or partisan delaying tactics,' Byrd said as he fumbled through his pockets for his copy of the Constitution. 'The Senate's role of advice and consent to presidential nominations is not a ceremonial exercise.'

Source: **www.washingtonpost.com**, page A6, 26 January 2005

Confirming a secretary of state, he said, 'was designed to be a constitutional duty, not a political fundraising opportunity'.

Alberto Gonzales was, like Condoleezza Rice, looking to move from a White House post in the first term to a cabinet department in the second. And his critics believed that he, like Dr Rice, was too much of a loyalist to the President to be an effective cabinet officer. 'It's hard to be a straight shooter when you're a blind loyalist,' commented New York Democrat Senator Charles Schumer. The 18-member Senate Judiciary Committee split 10–8 along party lines in their recommendatory vote on Mr Gonzales. After a 3-day debate on the Senate floor, Mr Gonzales was confirmed by a 60–36 vote margin (see Table 1.3). The 'yes' votes were made up of 54 Republicans joined by 6 Democrats — all regarded as moderates, such as Mary Landrieu of Louisiana, Joseph Lieberman of Connecticut and Ben Nelson of Nebraska.

Post	New cabinet officer	Senate vote
Secretary of State	Condoleezza Rice	85–13
Secretary of Agriculture	Michael Johanns	Voice vote
Attorney General	Alberto Gonzales	60–36
Secretary of Commerce	Carlos Gutierrez	Voice vote
Secretary of Health and Human Services	Michael Leavitt	Voice vote
Secretary of Education	Margaret Spellings	Voice vote
Secretary of Energy	Samuel Bodman	Voice vote
Secretary of Veterans' Affairs	Jim Nicholson	Voice vote
Secretary of Homeland Security	Michael Chertoff	98–0

Table 1.3 Senate confirmation votes of second-term cabinet officers

A cabinet 'that looks like America'

President-elect Bill Clinton famously remarked in 1992 that he wanted a cabinet 'that looked like America'. In saying this, he was announcing that he was looking to appoint a diverse cabinet, especially as regards gender and race. During his two terms, Clinton made 29 cabinet appointments which included 5 women, 7 African-Americans, 3 Hispanics (one of them named to two posts) and 1 Asian-American.

Of the 24 cabinet appointments that George W. Bush has made thus far, 5 have been women, 4 African-Americans, 3 Hispanics and 2 Asian-Americans. In other words, Bush has equalled and may even have exceeded Clinton in the diversity of his cabinet. For the first time ever, the USA has both a Secretary of State and an Attorney General who come from ethnic minority groups — and one of them is also a woman. 'There has been an effort by the President to reach out and ensure that his staff and his team reflect the diversity of our country,' commented presidential adviser Dan Bartlett. 'Reach out and ensure diversity' is not normal Republican Party language. As in so many things, George W. Bush turns out to be something of a surprise.

When and why to hold a cabinet meeting

Bush's cabinet has also been unusual with regard to the frequency with which cabinet meetings were held during his first term. Whereas for most modern presidents the number of cabinet meetings declined markedly as the administration progressed, this did not occur during the first term of George W. Bush. Nor did the Bush presidency begin with the holding of frequent cabinet meetings. Both these factors are shown in Table 1.4. George W. Bush rejected the cabinet meeting formula used by predecessors such as Jimmy Carter and Ronald Reagan, both of whom began with very frequent cabinet meetings, a frequency that soon tailed off as the administration progressed.

	Number of cabinet meetings held			
President	**First year**	**Second year**	**Third year**	**Fourth year**
Jimmy Carter	36	23	9	6
Ronald Reagan	36	21	12	12
George W. Bush	9	5	8	6

Table 1.4 Frequency of cabinet meetings: Carter, Reagan and George W. Bush compared

Whereas Carter and Reagan both held 36 cabinet meetings in their first year in office, George W. Bush held only 9. In an interview early in Bush's first term, the then Secretary to the Cabinet, Albert Hawkins, commented that the President would not be overly influenced by media expectations into holding meetings that were not useful, describing Bush as 'a business executive' who is 'not overly devoted to "process"'. Indeed, Hawkins rightly predicted as early as February 2001 that 'there will be few cabinet meetings'. Instead, explained Hawkins, 'the President will call in cabinet officers for one-on-one meetings and will pick up the phone and call them'.

There are many reasons for a president to hold cabinet meetings: to check up on legislation currently going through Congress; to see people he would not otherwise see; to find out what is going on in the executive departments whose heads attend the meetings; and to sort out interdepartmental disputes, to name but four. But for George W. Bush, the cabinet meeting is a kind of 'team talk' — a chance for him to address the team on big-picture items. By using cabinet meetings in this way, he avoids the pitfalls of many of his predecessors. They often used cabinet meetings for detailed policy discussion. But as cabinet officers are policy *specialists* rather than the policy *generalists* who gather at UK cabinet meetings — and there is no doctrine of collective responsibility — many cabinet members went away from presidential cabinet meetings having been bored to tears by policy discussions of which they had no knowledge and even less interest.

The White House website (**www.whitehouse.gov**) shows when cabinet meetings are held and what is discussed. Both the first two cabinet meetings of 2005 were held to discuss the federal budget — a topic in which all cabinet officers would clearly have a keen interest. Further cabinet meetings were held just before and just after the congressional summer recess (see Table 1.5). The meeting on 6 September 2005 — the fourth of the year — was held to discuss the aftermath of Hurricane Katrina in the Gulf Coast states of Louisiana, Mississippi and Alabama, and specifically to address the criticism levelled at the federal government over its slow response to the damage to and flooding of New Orleans.

Date of cabinet meeting	Topics discussed
7 February	The budget
5 April	The budget passage in Congress
13 July	Economy, energy, trade
6 September	Aftermath of Hurricane Katrina

Table 1.5 Cabinet meetings, 2005

At the end of a cabinet meeting, Bush has initiated the practice of inviting members of the White House press corps into the cabinet room for a brief photo opportunity and a statement from the President, followed by a brief question-and-answer session. At the end of Bush's first 2005 cabinet meeting — held on 7 February — he made the following remarks to the press assembled round the perimeter of the cabinet room:

> This is my first cabinet meeting of the year 2005. I welcomed new members of our cabinet to the table and congratulated them on their confirmations.

> Today we discussed a lot of issues. I reminded them that the war on terror goes on, but mainly we discussed the budget. We're submitting our budget [to Congress] today. It is a budget that sets priorities. Our priorities are winning the war on terror, protecting our homeland, growing our economy.

In the question-and-answer session with the press that followed his statement, the President took questions on the Middle East and the likelihood of Congress passing the budget — 'Well that's a great question!' began the President's answer to the latter.

The second cabinet meeting of the year came a couple of months later on 5 April, the day when members of Congress would return to Washington after their Easter recess. The real purpose of the meeting was to urge Congress to get on with finalising the budget by reconciling the House and Senate versions. The President, in his remarks to the press after the meeting, stated:

> I urge Congress to successfully conclude budget negotiations. The House [of Representatives] has passed the budget resolution; the Senate has passed the budget resolution. We look forward to working with the leadership to successfully conclude those negotiations. It's important that we get a budget which will show the American people that we will spend their money wisely.

Again, there was a particular event that triggered the holding of the meeting. In this sense, his meetings are far more predictable in terms of timing than those of any of his recent predecessors, who seemed to hold a meeting merely because there hadn't been one for some time. Bush cabinet meetings are often, as on this occasion, linked with events in Congress.

Bush also uses the press briefing after the cabinet meeting to praise his cabinet officers. At the 5 April briefing, Bush began his remarks thus:

> Just concluded the second cabinet meeting of the second term. I want to thank my cabinet officials for doing such a fine job. I appreciate your hard work, and thank you for your dedication to the country.

Such public ego stroking can go a long way in helping to build up cordiality and trust among a group that can all too easily feel isolated from the White House.

In his press briefing after the 6 September cabinet meeting in the wake of Hurricane Katrina, the President stated:

> My message to the cabinet this morning is this: this administration is not going to rest until every life can be saved; until families are reconnected; until this recovery is complete. Our immediate goals are these: we want to complete the search and recovery; we want to restore essential services; we want to drain the water in the affected areas and begin removing debris; and we are assessing public health and safety matters.

> I was briefed on plans to immediately help our folks; plans to reconnect families; plans to make sure healthcare is available — and [Health and Human Services] Secretary [Michael] Leavitt gave me a good brief; plans on housing, both immediate and long-term housing. Most importantly, I was briefed by members of my cabinet about how we're going to make sure that people who are owed a Social Security cheque get their Social Security cheque. A lot of people are doing good work. We've got a heck of a lot more work to do, and that's exactly what this government is going to do.

Clearly, the purpose of holding the cabinet meeting on that September morning was for the President to be briefed and for him to reassure Americans that his administration was focused on bringing speedy relief to the hurricane-stricken areas of the southern USA. In this sense, Bush's cabinet meetings fulfil another long-standing cabinet function — that of being a public relations exercise.

Is the cabinet still useful?

Presumably President George W. Bush would answer this question in the affirmative. We don't yet know what most of the Bush cabinet members think. We will have to wait for the memoirs to come. There is one verdict already in print — former Treasury Secretary Paul O'Neill's kiss-and-tell autobiography, somewhat curiously called *The Price of Loyalty*. In this book, published in 2004, O'Neill described George W. Bush at a cabinet meeting as being 'like a blind man in a room full of deaf people'. Not very complimentary. Nelson Polsby, the eminent political scientist and presidency-watcher, has recently stated that the trouble with being a member of the president's cabinet is that, although 'you get a seat at the table, the table doesn't get used!' Or not very often at least. Those like Condoleezza Rice, Alberto Gonzales and Margaret Spellings, who have swapped a White House office for the occasional visit to the cabinet room, will have a very good perspective on just how useful the institution is today.

Exercises

1. How does the turnover in President George W. Bush's cabinet compare with that of his predecessors?
2. Why and to what extent have recent presidents attempted to balance their cabinet in terms of race and gender?
3. What are the main reasons why presidents hold cabinet meetings?
4. What does Nelson Polsby mean by saying of the president's cabinet members that they 'get a seat at the table [but] the table doesn't get used'?

Chapter 2

Red and Blue America

Red vs blue on the map

Figure 2.1 represents the states of the USA won by Bush and Kerry in the 2004 presidential election. Republican (Bush) states are normally coloured red, while Democrat (Kerry) states usually appear in blue. Trying to cross America from east to west on such a map is rather like trying to cross the Red Sea! From Florida in the southeast to Ohio in the upper Midwest, from Idaho in the northwest to Arizona in the desert southwest, it's just one unbroken swathe of red. And Kerry's troops, in trying to cross this Red Sea, suffered a not dissimilar fate to the Egyptians in the Old Testament story. They were drowned! The Democrats have just three blue peninsulas left: the northeast, the Great Lakes and the west coast.

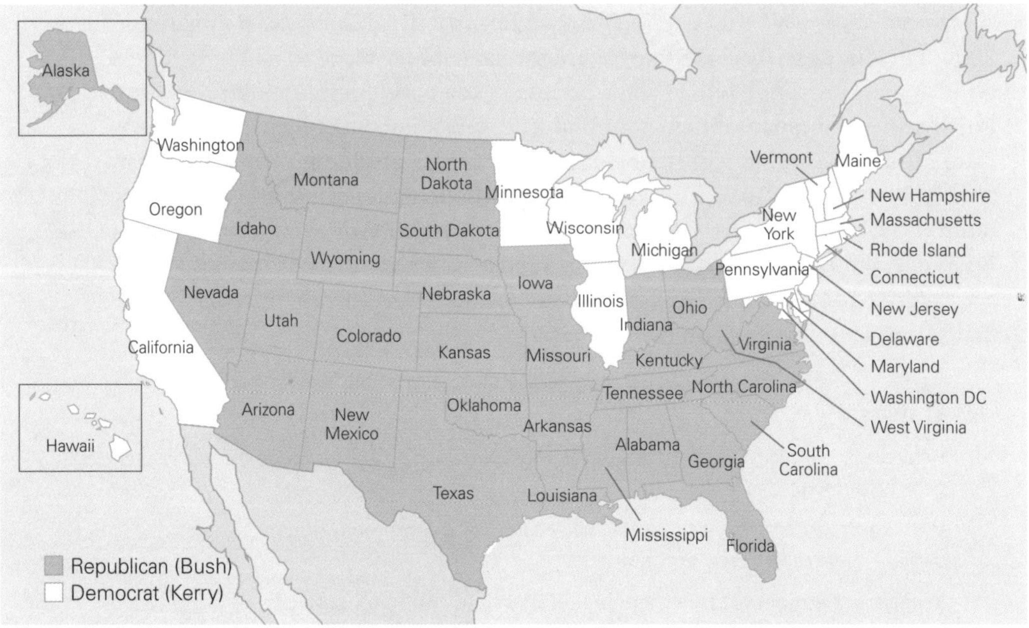

Figure 2.1 States won by Bush and Kerry in the presidential election, 2004

After the 2000 elections, it became part of conventional wisdom that the USA was a 49–49 nation. In the 2000 presidential election, both major party candidates ended up with around 49% of the popular vote. The Electoral College divided 271–267. In the House of Representatives it was 221–212 with

2 independents, while the Senate split exactly 50–50. In 2004, things swung a fraction in the Republicans' favour: 51–48% in the popular vote; 286–252 in the Electoral College; 232–202 in the House; 55–45 in the Senate. In the presidential election, only three states changed hands from 2000 — New Mexico, New Hampshire and Iowa. New Mexico, which in 2000 was a solitary island of blue in the 'Red Sea', switched to the Republicans. New Hampshire, which in 2000 was a solitary piece of red in the blue northeast, switched to the Democrats. And the Republicans enticed Iowa away from the Democrats' Great Lakes peninsula. In other words, the 2004 electoral map looks even more tribal than did the one 4 years earlier.

And so the USA is portrayed as two rival societies: Red America versus Blue America. Red America is rather more male than female. It is overwhelmingly white, although in certain areas it is increasingly Hispanic. It is overwhelmingly Protestant (and specifically, evangelical), but has been joined of late by practising Catholics. It is wealthy, rural or suburban, and unmistakably conservative. In Red America, the most significant issues in 2004 were moral issues and terrorism. They love George and Laura; they loathe Bill and Hillary. Britton Stein of Sugar Land, Texas describes George W. Bush as 'a man, a man's man, a manly man'. Al Gore, on the other hand, was 'a ranting and raving little whiny baby'.

By contrast, Blue America is more female than male. It is still a rainbow coalition of white, black, Asian and Hispanic. Churchgoing is not that important in Blue America. It is less wealthy, predominantly urban and unmistakably liberal. In Blue America, the most significant issues in 2004 were the economy, jobs and the war in Iraq — of which they disapproved. Some of them still love Bill and Hillary; they mostly loathe George and Laura. Tom Harrison of San Francisco describes Bill Clinton as 'intelligent', 'charismatic' and 'a good representation of America'. George W. Bush, on the other hand, is 'frightening', 'a total imbecile' and a 'monkey boy'.

The trouble is that this is a hopeless caricature of US politics. Believe it at your peril!

Differing shades of purple

Table 2.1 considers each state not only in terms of which party won it in the 2004 presidential election, but also in terms of major party representation in Congress, as well as party control of the state governorship and state legislature. It shows that only 11 of the 50 states can in any true sense be described as 'red' or 'blue'. In these 11 states, one party not only won the presidential election in that state, but also currently holds both Senate seats and controls the House delegation, the state governorship and the two houses of the state legislature. And it's quite a surprising list. Both Missouri and Ohio are generally considered key battleground states in a presidential election. Indeed,

Rank	State	Presidential vote, 2004	Senate	House	State governor	State legislature
1	**Alaska**	R	RR	R	R	RR
	Idaho	R	RR	R	R	RR
3	**Georgia**	R	RR	R	R	RR
	Missouri	R	RR	R	R	RR
	Ohio	R	RR	R	R	RR
	South Carolina	R	RR	R	R	RR
	Texas	R	RR	R	R	RR
	Utah	R	RR	R	R	RR
9	Arizona	R	RR	R	D	RR
	Florida	R	RD	R	R	RR
	Indiana	R	RD	R	R	RR
	Kansas	R	RR	R	D	RR
	Kentucky	R	RR	R	R	RD
	Virginia	R	RR	R	D	RR
	Wyoming	R	RR	R	D	RR
16	Nebraska	R	RD	R	R	–
17	Alabama	R	RR	R	R	DD
	Nevada	R	RD	R	R	RD
	New Hampshire	D	RR	R	D	RR
	Oklahoma	R	RR	R	D	DR
	Pennsylvania	D	RR	R	D	RR
	South Dakota	R	RD	D	R	RR
23	Iowa	R	RD	R	D	=R
	Mississippi	R	RR	=	R	DD
25	Colorado	R	RD	R	R	DD
	North Carolina	R	RR	R	D	DD
	North Dakota	R	DD	D	R	RR
	Tennessee	R	RR	D	D	RD
29	Minnesota	D	DR	=	R	DR
	Montana	R	RD	R	D	D=
31	Louisiana	R	DR	R	D	DD
	Michigan	D	DD	R	D	RR
	New Mexico	R	RD	R	D	DD
34	Wisconsin	D	DD	=	D	RR
35	Arkansas	R	DD	D	R	DD
	Connecticut	D	DD	R	R	DD
	Delaware	D	DD	R	D	DR
	Maine	D	RR	D	D	DD
	New York	D	DD	D	R	RD
	Oregon	D	DR	D	D	DR
	Rhode Island	D	DR	D	R	DD
42	California	D	DD	D	R	DD
	Hawaii	D	DD	D	R	DD
	Maryland	D	DD	D	R	DD
	Massachusetts	D	DD	D	R	DD
	Vermont	D	DI	I	R	DD
	West Virginia	R	DD	D	D	DD
48	**Illinois**	D	DD	D	D	DD
	New Jersey	D	DD	D	D	DD
	Washington	D	DD	D	D	DD

Note: R = Republican; D = Democrat; I = Independent. All states except Nebraska have bicameral state legislatures. Nebraska's unicameral state legislature is also non-partisan. The symbol '=' indicates that the delegation is divided equally between the two major parties.

Table 2.1 States ranked according to level of Republican Party support, 2004

Missouri is the most reliable bellwether state, having voted for the winner in the presidential election in each of the last 12 elections. Ohio voted for Bush over Kerry by only 120,000 votes in 2004.

The map with which we started would tell us, for example, that West Virginia is a red state. But both its senators are Democrats. Its 3-member state delegation in the House of Representatives includes 2 Democrats. It has a Democrat governor and the Democrats control both houses of the state legislature. On the other hand, we are told that Pennsylvania is a blue state. Yet both its senators are Republicans. Its 19-member state delegation in the House of Representatives includes 12 Republicans. The Republicans also control both houses of the state legislature. And the same kind of things could be said of other states, such as Arkansas, Louisiana, New Mexico or New Hampshire.

Three blue states — Maine, New Hampshire and Pennsylvania — are represented in the Senate by two Republican senators. Likewise, red state Arkansas is represented by two Democrat senators. Twenty-one states have a state governor of a different party from the way the state voted in the 2004 presidential election. There are 12 red states with a Democrat governor and 9 blue states with a Republican governor. And the blue states with Republican governors include California, New York and Massachusetts, all of which would be on most people's list of the bluest states. Except in a few ideologically homogeneous states such as Alaska and Idaho, it's not so much red and blue as differing shades of purple.

In their recent book, *Red over Blue: The 2004 Elections and American Politics* (Rowman and Littlefield, 2005), James Ceaser and Andrew Busch comment:

> In some presentations, the red–blue divide is evoked to express the idea of a radically polarized society split between two conflicting ways of life: a red America that is small-town, religious, and dominated by the church steeple, and a blue America that is secular, urban and dominated by Thai restaurants. And in the most facile characterizations, everyone living in the first kind of area is imagined to vote Republican, while everyone in the second votes Democratic. It is as if Republicans and Democrats never meet, except perhaps in a chance encounter at an airport.

Or take this from a *Washington Post* report just after the 2004 election:

> When Blue Americans and Red Americans talk about each other, a fundamental disagreement has to do with which side is trying to ruin the other side's life. At the risk of oversimplifying, many Blue Americans believe that Bush voters are trying to shove conservative morals into liberal bedrooms, to mandate prayer before intercourse and replace Victoria's Secret with Gladys's Nightshirts. Conversely, many Red Americans believe that liberals seek the spread of promiscuity and license into every village and they won't be truly happy until vibrators are distributed in junior high schools.

But the danger is that if we look at US politics through the prism of the red–blue debate, we may miss some of the more important things that are happening.

Key word

Bible Belt: an area of the USA that includes much of the southern and some of the Midwestern states in which Bible-based, evangelical, Protestant Christianity is predominant. It stretches from Texas, north to Kansas, east to Virginia and south to mid-Florida (see Figure 2.2).

Purple in practice

Observers wedded too much to the red–blue divide might have run off with the idea that George W. Bush won re-election in 2004 merely by mobilising core Republican voters in Red America. They may also have been persuaded by much media commentary — erroneous, in my view — that Bush's re-election was largely courtesy of evangelical Christians, who were even more motivated to vote in states that offered them a chance to vote on a state constitutional amendment to ban gay marriage. It was 'moral issues' wot won it!

But where did Bush increase his vote most significantly? Not in Michigan (+0.5%), Ohio (+0.5%), Montana (+1%) or North Dakota (+2%). All these states saw an increase in Bush's vote of less than the national average. Yet all four had an anti-gay marriage amendment on the ballot. The states where Bush *really* increased his vote, thus helping to bump up his share of the popular vote from 49% to 52%, were Hawaii (+8%), Rhode Island (+7%), Connecticut (+6%), New Jersey (+6%) and New York (+5%). Not exactly the **Bible Belt**, is it? All are blue states and none offered a vote on gay marriage. Despite the disputed (2000) election, 9/11, the wars in Afghanistan and Iraq, and even Michael Moore's attempts to hot up the cultural wars, US voters were less divided in 2004 than they had been in 2000.

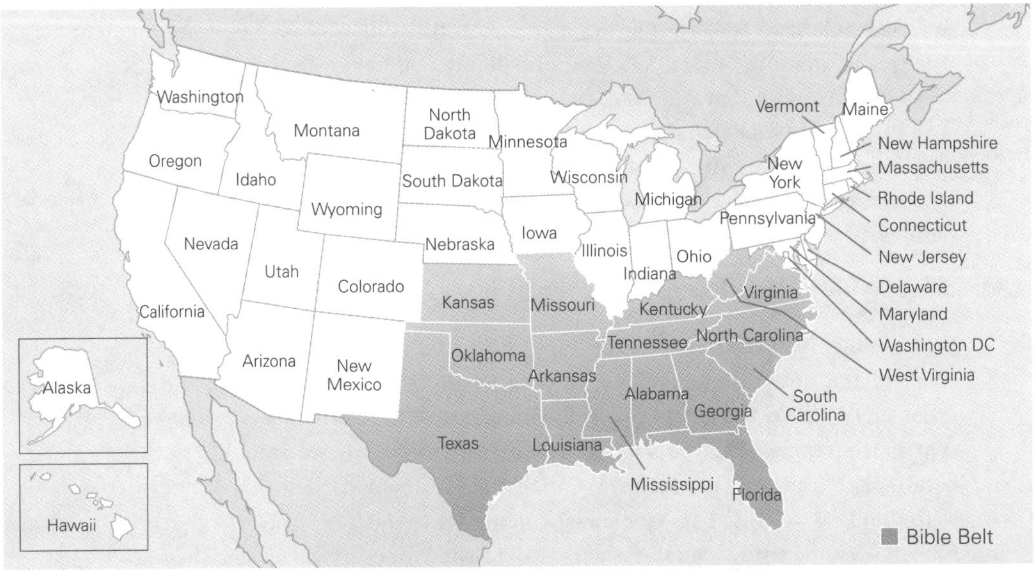

Figure 2.2 The Bible Belt (shaded area)

Or take another example. Commentators are often telling us how partisan and divided Congress is these days. True, the figures on partisan voting in Congress during the third year of Bush's first term did show some significant increase. But in neither house did the figures reach the level of partisanship seen during 1995 when Democrat President Bill Clinton faced the first year of the Republican majority in Congress trying to pass its ***Contract with America*** items (see Table 2.2). And the 2004 figures showed the levels of partisanship in both houses in decline — very significantly in the House of Representatives. Again, this is evidence of more purple than blue and red.

Key word

Contract with America: the Republican Party policy document that was behind the party's campaign to win control of the House of Representatives in the 1994 mid-term elections.

Year	House votes	Senate votes
1995	73	69
1996	56	62
1997	50	50
1998	56	56
1999	47	63
2000	43	49
2001	55	40
2002	43	45
2003	52	67
2004	47	52

Table 2.2 Party votes as a proportion of all recorded votes in Congress, 1995–2004 (%)

Understanding Red America

But having said all that, there is still a discernible swathe of the USA that is Red America. During 2005, the *Washington Post* sent reporter David Von Drehle, along with a photographer and his assistant, to drive from Lincoln, Nebraska, south for around 700 miles to Waco, Texas. The four states they travelled through are all red states — Nebraska, Kansas, Oklahoma and Texas (see Figure 2.3). On the 2004 electoral map, they were about as far from Blue America as you can get.

In his subsequent article, Von Drehle stated that the first thing that strikes you about Red America is its geography. Whereas Blue America is characterised by the height of the buildings in the big cities of New York, Boston or Chicago, Red America is characterised by vast horizons, flatness and space. 'I like driving where I am the only one on the road,' said Paul Kern in Waco, Nebraska, where on average there is just one person per square mile. (In Manhattan, there are 50,000 people per square mile.) He continued: 'I like being able to shout and have nobody hear me. I like to be able to throw a snowball as far as I can and not hit anybody or anything.'

The second thing that strikes you about much of Red America is its ethnic uniformity — its sameness. According to the Census Bureau, York County,

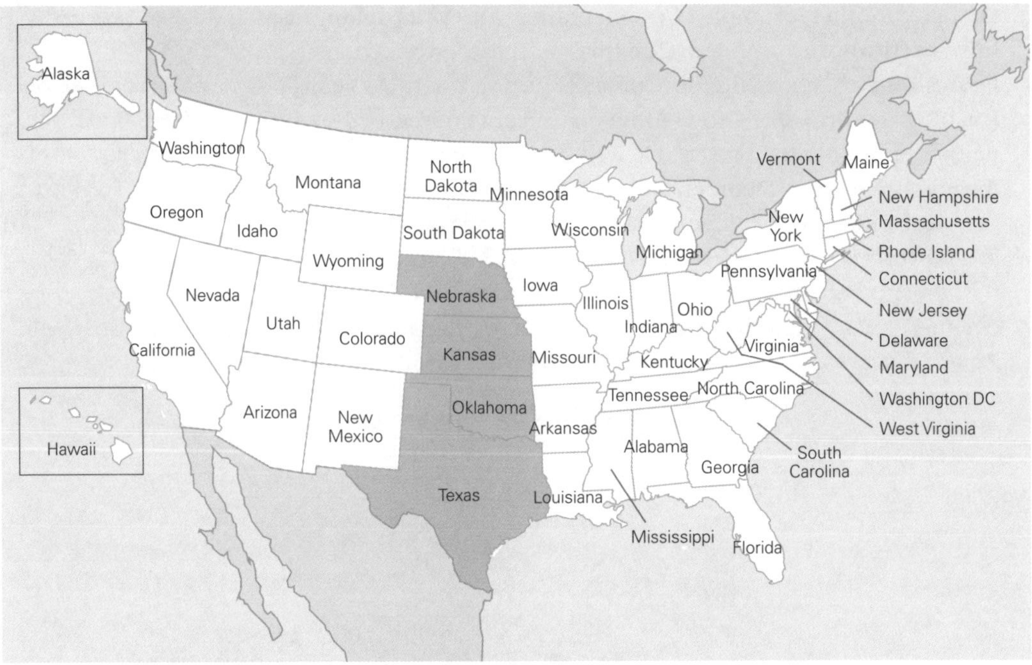

Figure 2.3 The USA, showing Nebraska, Kansas, Oklahoma and Texas

Nebraska — in which Waco is situated — is 97% white and more than 98% US-born.

It's a pretty safe place to live. 'Where else do you have a place where you don't have to worry about crime, about juvenile delinquency, where you can leave your doors unlocked?' Kern asked the *Post* reporter. (Certainly not in Manhattan, or in Washington DC.)

It's also a pretty cheap place to live compared with Blue America. In York, Nebraska, Von Drehle found 62 houses for sale, but only one cost more than $200,000 (£112,000). The stories that Nebraskans hear of their members of Congress struggling to live on $150,000 (£84,000) a year in Washington simply astounds them. 'I'd own this whole town with that kind of money!' Kern claimed. 'I could live like a king.'

God appears to be very prominent in Red America. Conversations about religious faith proceed a bit awkwardly — if at all — in Blue America. But in Red America, folk are as comfortable with the subject of religion as they are with the weather. Even on weekdays, church parking lots will be full of cars. The *Oklahoman* — the largest state-wide newspaper of Oklahoma — prints 'Today's Prayer' on its front page. (You won't find 'Today's Prayer' in the *New York Times* or the *Washington Post*.) And two of the most prominent high-rise office buildings in downtown Oklahoma City light their windows at night to make the shape of a cross.

Why the red–blue divide?

US politics in the 1950s, 1960s and 1970s was said to be all about bipartisanship. There were liberal Democrats and conservative Democrats; there were conservative Republicans and moderate Republicans. The two major parties were largely non-ideological and both encompassed a huge philosophical range. In the Democratic Party you had liberals like John Kennedy and Hubert Humphrey. But you also had (at least until 1964) conservatives like Strom Thurmond and, even later, George Wallace. In the Republican Party, you had conservatives such as Barry Goldwater but also moderates like Nelson Rockefeller.

Conservative Democrats are nowadays an endangered species. They have died, retired or joined the Republican Party. Likewise, moderate Republicans are becoming increasingly scarce. Senator James Jeffords of Vermont, who jumped ship to become an independent in 2001, spent the last 5 years voting mostly with the Democrats but will retire at the end of the 2006 Congress. Commentators tell us that the US political parties are becoming more ideologically cohesive. The old 'coalition' parties seem to be disappearing. Why? There are four reasons worthy of serious consideration — all things that have occurred from the 1980s up to the present day.

The first thing that happened was Ronald Reagan. Previous Republican presidents — Eisenhower (1953–61), Nixon (1969–74) and Ford (1974–77) — governed essentially as centrists. Reagan was clearly more ideological. He wooed conservatives away from the Democratic Party, while making it uncomfortable for moderates to remain in the Republican Party.

The second thing that happened was the end of the Cold War. From 1941 to the end of the 1980s, the two major parties looked so ideologically similar because they both accepted the foreign policy consensus — the need for unity in the face of the threat from the Soviet Union. The collapse of the Soviet Union ended the need for that consensus.

The third thing that happened was Bill Clinton. The Clinton years are something of a paradox, for although Clinton ran as a 'New Democrat' and sometimes adopted Republican policies and themes ('the era of big government is over'), his presidency proved highly divisive. Clinton, the first baby boomer president, reopened the divisive issues of the 1960s — sex, the role of women and the nature of authority and morality.

And while all this was going on, a fourth factor — technology — happened. Direct mail, talk radio, cable television, mobile phones, e-mail and the internet all enabled ideological soul mates not only to communicate with each other more effectively, but also to evangelise. These 'new media' are quickly replacing the 'old media' — newspapers, journals (*Time*, *Newsweek* etc.) and network television (ABC, CBS, NBC) — as the shaper of public opinion. What this means is that, while Americans used to read, hear and see a spectrum of comment, now they tend to tune in to or log on to the channel or the website that reinforces their existing views.

What next?

Given these causes, what is likely to happen in the coming decades? There is no doubt that both Bill Clinton and George W. Bush have been 'dividers' rather than 'uniters'. Clinton's scandals were always going to make him unacceptable in Red America. George W. Bush, on the other hand, became divisive more as a result of the closeness and controversy of the 2000 election. Many in Blue America saw him as having 'stolen' the election and therefore as 'illegitimate'. The events of 9/11 lessened those feelings, but only temporarily. The military operations in Afghanistan and especially in Iraq made Bush the Divider in Chief. If the Democrats nominate Hillary Clinton as their presidential candidate in 2008, expect the divide to continue.

It seems unlikely that the 'war on terror' will become a force for unity in the way that the Cold War was for much of the latter half of the twentieth century. It is too closely bound up with the events in Iraq. Were the USA to become subject to further acts of domestic terrorism, divisions would probably lessen. Bill Clinton's most uniting moment was undoubtedly his reaction to the Oklahoma City bombing, just as George W. Bush's was his reaction to 9/11. But that would be a big price to pay for political consensus.

It also seems highly unlikely that the technological revolution is going to go into reverse. One must therefore presume that many Americans will continue to view their politics in monocolour, so to speak: red for *Fox News*; blue for the *Drudge Report*.

In the meantime, it is worth remembering that US politics is a bit more than just red and blue. In 2004, John Kerry won 75% of the vote in the 30th District of red state Texas — that's downtown Dallas — and Bush won 68% of the vote in the 22nd District of blue state California — the city of Bakersfield. So when talking red and blue, don't forget the shades of purple.

Exercises

1. Which are the USA's most 'red states' and most 'blue states'?
2. Give three examples of what might be called 'purple states' and explain why they fall within that category.
3. In which states did George W. Bush gain the largest increase in his share of the vote from the 2000 to the 2004 elections, and what 'colour' are these states?
4. Explain five characteristics of 'Red America'.
5. What four factors does the author give for the rise of the red–blue divide in US politics?
6. Explain the reasons why the author believes this red–blue divide is likely to continue in US politics.

Chapter 3

George W. Bush's first term

First assessments

It is rumoured that on the day that the storming of the Bastille occurred in 1789 to herald the beginning of the French Revolution and the end of his reign, Louis XVI wrote in his diary — presumably in French — 'Nothing much happened today.' I mention this to illustrate how tricky first assessments can be when we are standing too close to the events. To put it another way, political commentary is an activity better conducted with a telescope than a magnifying glass. Thus there is considerable danger in trying to assess a presidency which, at the time of writing, is likely to be only just over half way through. This might be even truer when we consider how problematic second-term presidencies can often be — think Nixon and Watergate, Reagan and Iran–Contra, Clinton and Lewinsky. Michael Howard's comment during the recent UK general election campaign about football teams that are ahead at half-time is well taken — though not in Mr Howard's case. Nonetheless, let's see what we can make of the George W. Bush presidency at half-time.

Four years of memorable dates

If one wanted to sum up the George W. Bush first term as a series of dates then the following would provide a succinct summary: 12/12, 9/11, 4/9, 12/13, 11/2 — remembering that Americans always put the month first and the day second. The first date is 12 December 2000 — the day on which the US Supreme Court ended the election recount in Florida and effectively handed the presidency to George W. Bush. The second date needs no explanation. The third is 9 April 2003 — the day on which Baghdad was captured by the US-led coalition forces. The fourth is 13 December 2003 — the day on which Saddam Hussein was captured. The fifth is 2 November 2004 — the day on which George W. Bush defeated John Kerry.

But, of course, it is 9/11 — 11 September 2001 — which captures all one really needs to know about these 4 years. It transformed the man, his presidency and possibly the world. For the USA this date will stand alongside 4 July 1776 (the Declaration of Independence) and 7 December 1941 (Pearl Harbor) as dates that changed the nation.

Chapter 3

The first 234 days

11 September 2001 was the 234th day of the presidency of George W. Bush. He had fought the 2000 election campaign proclaiming himself to be 'a uniter, not a divider' — a clear reference to his predecessor, who had been such a divisive character, not least during the whole torment of impeachment. But this hope was doomed from the start by the nature of the election and how it was eventually resolved by the Supreme Court on 12 December 2000. Exactly 5 weeks earlier, Bush had lost the nationwide popular vote to Al Gore, but in the Electoral College it was Bush who seemed to have won — that is, if he could keep hold of the Electoral College votes of Florida.

When on 12 December the Supreme Court made a 7–2 ruling that the Florida recount was unconstitutional and then a 5–4 ruling that all time had expired to find any other remedy, George W. Bush became the true president-elect and the third successive president to fail to gain 50% of the popular vote. Democrats were outraged. Bush was an 'accidental president'. To some, this was a 'stolen election'. Some reworded the presidential anthem 'Hail to the Chief' as 'Hail to the *Thief*'. (For Nixon back in 1974, it had been 'Jail to the Chief'!) But Republicans too were unhappy with what they saw as mean-spirited tactics deployed by many Democrats. They redesigned the blue 'Gore–Lieberman' badges to read 'Sore Loserman'.

Democrats and Republicans alike were expecting Bush's to be a domestic presidency. The former Texas governor had no foreign policy experience. Certainly, had Americans been looking for a foreign policy president in 2000, they would have chosen Al Gore, not George W. Bush. But only 12% of voters told exit pollsters that foreign policy or national security was their number one issue. During the 2000 campaign Bush talked of a 'humble' foreign policy — whatever that meant.

Bush had received a number of plaudits for an effective transition — one that was certainly more orderly than that of Bill Clinton in 1992–93. Bush's cabinet nominations had generally been regarded as competent and uncontroversial. But even in these first 8 months there were some surprises. Following the closeness and controversial nature of the election, most commentators were expecting Bush to govern as a leader of some grand, national coalition characterised by bipartisanship and compromise. But Bush immediately pressed ahead with his conservative agenda — tax cuts and education reform. Bush was also more adept at relations with Congress than his critics and opponents had expected. He courted leading congressional Democrats. Among the first dining guests at the White House were Ted Kennedy and his wife. Kennedy's post-dinner comment that Bush would be 'difficult to deal with' because 'he's so damn genial' proved to be accurate. One Democrat House member was heard to remark that 'it's strange to have a president who knows his manners'. The *New York Times* — not known as a fan of George W. Bush — was moved to comment: 'Even Mr Bush's opponents would have to acknowledge he has shown far more skill in handling Congress than many expected.'

Bush moved quickly on his first major piece of legislation — a $1.35 trillion tax cut. It passed the House by 240–154 and the Senate by 58–33. Those supporting the tax cut included 28 House Democrats and 12 Senate Democrats.

But no sooner had this triumph been achieved than Senator James Jeffords of Vermont announced that he was leaving the Republican Party and would sit as an independent. Party defections are never good news, but this one was especially devastating because the Jeffords defection handed control of the Senate to the Democrats. Having enjoyed control of the White House and both houses of Congress for the first time in nearly 50 years, the Republicans lost the Senate after less than 6 months. There was every reason to believe that Bush would now face divided government for at least the next $3\frac{1}{2}$ years.

In his first inaugural address on 20 January 2001, President Bush had quoted Thomas Jefferson in an attempt to assure a divided nation that a US president — even one whose election had been the subject of considerable dispute, as was Jefferson's — has help from above in troubled times. 'We know the race is not to the swift, nor the battle to the strong,' Bush said on that raw, cold January day. 'Do you not think an angel rides in the whirlwind and directs this storm?' It took just 234 days for the whirlwind to strike the presidency of George W. Bush.

That fateful day

In the early days of September 2001, the noted political commentator Haynes Johnson published his thirteenth book. It was a critique of the Clinton years entitled *The Best of Times* (Harcourt, 2001). In the Preface, he wrote:

> My story involves America at its zenith, a society so favoured as it entered a new millennium that its people could be excused for believing they were experiencing their very best of times. Looking to the future, America's prospects appeared unlimited. They enjoyed unprecedented peace and prosperity. After the global terrors and tragedies into which they had been drawn throughout the 20th century, by the closing years of that epoch they faced no crises domestic or foreign. No threat of war existed. No new enemies challenged America.

I suspect that within a few days of his book's publication, Mr Johnson somewhat regretted those remarks.

On the morning of Tuesday, 11 September 2001, President Bush rose at 6.30 a.m. to take a 4-mile run along the deserted beach of Longboat Key, Florida. Many members of the President's cabinet were also out of Washington that morning. Attorney General John Ashcroft was on his way to a meeting in

Milwaukee, Wisconsin. The Chairman of the Joint Chiefs of Staff, General Hugh Shelton, was heading east across the Atlantic in a plane bound for Europe. Secretary of State Colin Powell was in Lima, Peru, meeting with the country's new president, Alejandro Toledo. There were some administration members left in Washington. CIA Director George Tenet was breakfasting with former Oklahoma senator David Boren at the St Regis Hotel on the corner of 16th and K Streets, three blocks from the White House. Secretary of Defense Donald Rumsfeld was in his office at the Pentagon.

At 8.30 a.m., the President's motorcade left Longboat Key to drive the short distance to downtown Sarasota, where the President was due at a second-grade (7-year-olds) class at Emma E. Booker Elementary School. On his way to the school, the President was informed that a small, twin-engine plane had crashed into the New York World Trade Center's North Tower, in what appeared to be an accident. 'The pilot must have had a heart attack,' responded the President.

At 9.05 a.m. — just 2 minutes after United Airlines Flight 175 had crashed into the South Tower — White House Chief of Staff Andrew Card whispered into the President's right ear as he sat in front of the second-grade class: 'A second plane hit the second tower. America is under attack.' At almost the same moment, an aide approached George Tenet's breakfast table at the St Regis Hotel in Washington DC: 'Mr Director, there's a serious problem.' In Lima, Peru, Colin Powell heard the news. 'Get the plane. Go tell them we're leaving.'

Around 20 minutes later, Secret Service agents burst in to Vice-President Dick Cheney's West Wing office. 'Sir, we have to leave immediately.' Without waiting for a response, the agents grabbed Cheney under his arms, virtually lifting him off the ground as they propelled him out of his office into the White House basement to a secure underground bunker.

Two minutes later, Donald Rumsfeld felt his Pentagon office shudder. He looked out of the window to see smoke pouring from one of the wings of the building.

There is a photograph of Andrew Card whispering those fateful words into the President's ear. The President looks awestruck. For the next few hours, Bush hop-scotched around the USA on Air Force One before returning to Washington once it was deemed safe enough for him to do so. That evening, he addressed the nation from the Oval Office. The words were gritty and determined, but his voice echoed his shocked appearance.

Three days later, Bush had found his voice. First, at a nationally televised prayer service in Washington's National Cathedral, he exhibited steely resolve:

> War has been waged against us by stealth and deceit and murder. This nation is peaceful, but fierce when stirred to anger. This conflict was begun on the timing and terms of others. It will end in a way and at an hour of our choosing.

Then at Ground Zero in New York came a moment that perhaps more than any other spoke for the whole Bush first term. Touring the scene of devastation, the President climbed onto some of the rubble where the World Trade Center had stood and began an impromptu speech to the rescue workers using a small megaphone. 'We can't hear you,' yelled a friendly voice from the crowd. The President responded: 'Well I hear you, the rest of the world hears you, and the people who knocked these buildings down will hear all of us soon.' As James Ceasar and Andrew Busch (*Red over Blue: The 2004 Elections and American Politics*, Rowman and Littlefield, 2005) commented: 'His relationship with the American people would never be the same'.

Six days later Bush was at it again, delivering a powerful speech to a joint session of Congress:

> Either you are with us, or you are with the terrorists. From this day forward, any nation that continues to harbour or support terrorism will be regarded by the United States as a hostile regime...Freedom and fear, justice and cruelty have always been at war, and we know that God is not neutral between them.

The political consequences

The immediate consequence of all this was that the President's approval rating shot up by over 40 percentage points. Congress worked with unusual speed to pass the Patriot Act before the end of October. The vote in the House was 357–66 and in the Senate an even more overwhelming 98–1. Bush used his political capital to move forward on his domestic agenda. His 'No Child Left Behind' education reform bill was passed with bipartisan support by mid-December. Indeed, Democrats liked it more than Republicans.

Within 6 weeks, Bush had dispatched 11,000 US troops to Afghanistan to root out the Taliban regime. He used his 2002 State of the Union Address to announce what would become known as 'the Bush doctrine' and the right to pre-emptive strikes. The same speech referred to Iraq, Iran and North Korea as having formed an 'axis of evil'.

With the Afghanistan campaign having been a speedy success, the President began to signal that Iraq was number two on his list. In early October 2002, with the mid-term elections just weeks away, votes were held in both houses of Congress to approve military action in Iraq. Democrats had been calling for authorisation votes and by doing so walked into a trap that Bush and the Republicans had laid for them. With US public opinion clearly supportive of military action in Iraq to remove Saddam Hussein's regime, it would be a brave member of Congress who would vote against supporting the President. The votes were overwhelmingly in favour of the President's position: 296–133 in the House and 77–23 in the Senate. The 77 senators voting 'yes' included the eventual Democratic Party presidential and vice-presidential candidates,

John Kerry and John Edwards — votes that would later make their opposition to the Iraq operation appear to be a policy flip-flop.

Mid-term successes

The Democrats went into the elections needing an overall gain of just 6 seats to add control of the House of Representatives to their control of the Senate, which they had gained the previous year. This was well within the average number of seats that the party not controlling the White House could expect to win in a mid-term election. But the Republicans went into the race with some considerable advantages.

First, the reapportionment following the 2000 census had awarded the red states (see Chapter 2) a net gain of 7 House seats. Second, the Republicans appeared better organised than the Democrats. They certainly had recruited some top-quality candidates, such as Senate candidates Elizabeth Dole in North Carolina and Norm Coleman in Minnesota. According to presidential watcher Michael Nelson, Bush threw himself into the mid-term elections 'earlier and more energetically than any president in history'. Just a year earlier, Democratic National Committee (DNC) Chairman Terry McAuliffe had claimed that Bush would 'be of no benefit to any Republican candidate in the country'. He could not have been more wrong. Bush held 70 fundraising events and raised a record $140 million, easily beating the previous record of $105 million set by Clinton in 1998. In the last 5 days of the campaign, the President travelled 10,000 miles, to 17 cities in 15 states. In some states — Georgia, for example — he clearly made the difference between victory and defeat for Republican candidates. And as the last stages of the campaign were being fought, the DNC had only $5 million to spend against the Republicans' $30 million.

The result was the first instance of the president's party gaining seats in both houses in a mid-term election since FDR's Democrats in 1934! Yet again, the Democrats had sorely underestimated George W. Bush.

The Iraq campaign

The first half of 2003 was dominated by events in Iraq. Bush allowed the moderates in his administration — led by Secretary of State Colin Powell — to make one final bid for United Nations support. But when it was not forthcoming, Bush led 'a coalition of the willing' instead. Military action began in Iraq on 20 March. Less than 3 weeks later — on 9 April — coalition troops arrived in the centre of Baghdad and toppled the statue of Saddam Hussein. On 2 May, a prematurely jubilant President Bush swept onto the aircraft carrier *USS Abraham Lincoln* and appeared under a huge banner that proclaimed: 'MISSION ACCOMPLISHED'. The President claimed that 'major combat operations in Iraq have ended'. It was just a pity that no one had informed the

Iraqi and foreign insurgents who continued to serve up a deadly routine of 'homicide bombings' on an almost daily basis for the remainder of the first term and beyond.

There was another burst of good news for the President on the eve of the presidential primary season when Saddam Hussein was captured on 13 December 2003. The situation in Iraq would feature as a major issue in the forthcoming presidential campaign — both in the Democratic primaries and later in the general election itself.

The era of big government returns

One of the most extraordinary facts about the Bush administration — a *Republican* administration — is its presiding over the largest overall increase in inflation-adjusted federal government spending since Lyndon Johnson's 'Great Society' programme of the mid-1960s. Even after excluding spending on defence and homeland security, Bush in his first term was the biggest-spending president in 30 years. Total federal government spending grew by 33% during his first term. The federal budget as a share of the economy grew from 18.5% of gross domestic product (GDP) on Clinton's last day in office to 20.3% by the end of Bush's first term. As Figure 3.1 shows, the total dollar increases in the federal budget grew dramatically during Bush's first term. And Figure 3.2 (overleaf) shows how big the federal budget has grown in relation to the economy as measured by GDP.

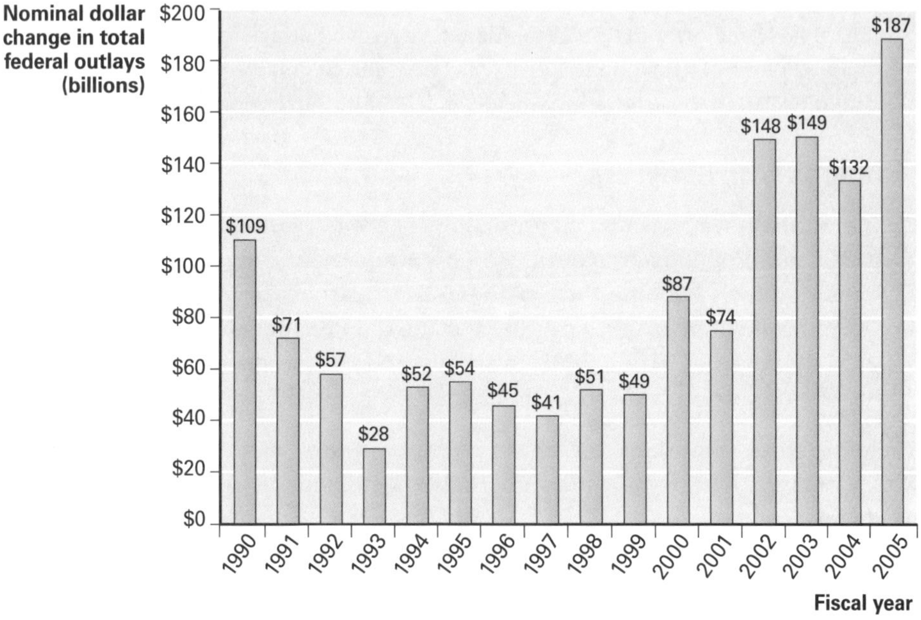

Source: Office of Management and Budget, *Historical Tables, Budget of the United States Government, Fiscal Year 2006*, Table 8.1, p. 125

Figure 3.1 The growth of federal government spending, 1990–2005

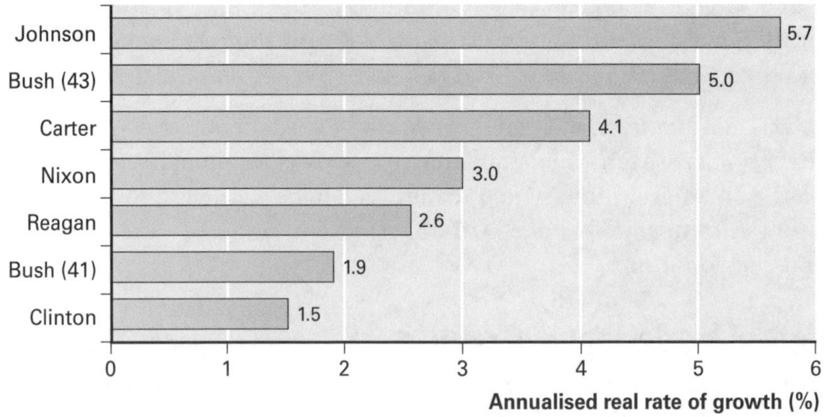

Source: (Slivinski's calculations) Based on data from Office of Management and Budget, *Historical Tables, Budget of the United States Government, Fiscal Year 2006,* Table 1.3, p. 25

Figure 3.2 Real annual growth rate of total government outlays by president

In an article in the 3 May 2005 edition of *Policy Analysis*, entitled 'The Grand Old Party: how Republicans became big spenders', Stephen Slivinski wrote:

> Once upon a time, the Republican Party frequently made the case for smaller government and occasionally backed up the rhetoric with action. Republicans won a historic electoral victory in 1994 partly by trumpeting their opposition to the big-spending congressional leadership and offering the alternative of balancing the budget by cutting spending. The first budget proposed by the Republican majority in 1995 eliminated three cabinet agencies and more than 200 federal programmes. Ten years later, the Republicans in Congress and the White House have become defenders of big government.

Relations with Congress

George W. Bush was an unusual president — he was a Republican who for the most part had Republican majorities in both houses of Congress. The House of Representatives remained under Republican Party control throughout the 4 years of his first term. As regards the Senate, the Republicans were in control for $2\frac{1}{2}$ of the 4 years. No Republican president in living memory had enjoyed this degree of party control in Congress.

There are three important matters to mention in looking at Bush's relations with Congress. The first is the remarkable fact that Bush became the first president not to use a veto during a full 4-year term since Martin van Buren (1837–41). Why was this? The President's supporters might suggest that his relations with Congress were so amenable that he had no need to use his veto power and that, anyway, his own party controlled Congress for most of his first term. These explanations are, I think, somewhat over-flattering to the President. I would also suggest that if the White House had truly believed this explanation, it would have made the veto-less first term something of a virtue in the President's re-election campaign. I never heard it mentioned. Although the presence of Republican majorities in Congress for much of the first term may be part of the reason, equally important in explaining this phenomenon is the President's very limited — some would say focused — policy agenda. To be somewhat blunt, if it's not tax cuts, the 'war on terror', faith-based initiatives or education, the President is not too bothered about it. He'll pretty much sign anything, even the Campaign Finance Reform Act (2002). Many conservative Republicans wished that their President *had* vetoed some of the big spending bills during these 4 years.

The second matter worthy of note is the stand-off between the President and Senate Democrats over his nominations to the federal courts, and the use by some Senate Democrats of the **filibuster** to stop nominees when they disapproved of their judicial philosophy — in other words, when they thought them too conservative. Of the President's 66 federal court nominations during his first term, only 35 (53%) were confirmed by the Senate. As Table 3.1 shows, this is well below the rate during previous administrations. Senate Democrats excused their tactics by pointing to Republican obstruction of many of President Clinton's court nominations during the period 1995–2001 when they controlled the Senate. While that is true, Table 3.1 shows that President Clinton enjoyed a far higher percentage of his court nominees being confirmed than has President Bush. Between 1946 and 2001, the average rate for the confirmation of federal court nominations during first terms was 84.3%. President Bush's rate of 53.0% compares very unfavourably with that. Senate Democrats would suggest that this President has tended to nominate more judges who are 'out of the mainstream' than did his predecessors.

Key word

filibuster: a device by which an individual senator, or a group of senators, can attempt to delay a bill or a nomination by using delaying tactics. It derives from senators' right of unlimited debate. A three-fifths vote (that is, 60 votes) is required to end a filibuster.

President	Judicial nominees confirmed during first term (%)
Harry Truman	90.9
Dwight Eisenhower	88.5
John Kennedy/Lyndon Johnson	82.8
Richard Nixon	92.7
Jimmy Carter	91.8
Ronald Reagan	78.6
George Bush	77.8
Bill Clinton	71.4
George W. Bush	53.0

***Table 3.1** Percentage of judicial nominees confirmed during presidential first terms, 1945–2005*

When Senate Republican Leader Bill Frist threatened to use the 'nuclear option' by changing the rules to make filibusters easier to stop, a group of 14 senators — 7 Democrats and 7 Republicans — made a pact not to support the use of filibusters for federal court nominations except under extraordinary circumstances. This so-called Gang of 14 was made up of mainly conservative Democrats and moderate Republicans, a number of whom find themselves facing the voters in 2006.

Thirdly, with regard to the **presidential support score**, President Bush rates highly compared with his recent predecessors. Indeed, as Table 3.2 shows, his 81.5% average support score is higher than any first-term presidents since the score was first published in 1953. Allowing for the vagaries of these statistics, Bush's is still quite a significant achievement. According to congressional scholar Norman Ornstein: 'Bush has confounded many of his critics with his ability to keep his party loyal and pass partisan initiatives while occasionally **reaching across the aisle** for a bipartisan achievement.'

Key words

presidential support score: an annual statistic that measures how often the president won in recorded votes in the House and Senate on which he took a clear position, expressed as a percentage of the whole.

reaching across the aisle: refers to the centre aisle that divides Republicans and Democrats in their semi-circular seating arrangements in both the House and Senate chambers. Thus to reach across the aisle is to seek support from both Republicans and Democrats in Congress.

President	Dates of first (or only) term	Average presidential support score (%)
Dwight Eisenhower	1953–57	78.1
Richard Nixon	1969–73	73.0
Jimmy Carter	1977–81	76.4
Ronald Reagan	1981–85	71.9
George Bush	1989–93	51.6
Bill Clinton	1993–97	66.1
George W. Bush	2001–05	81.5

Table 3.2 Average presidential support score for first-term presidents, 1953–2005

Getting re-elected

George W. Bush is the 43rd president of the USA, but he is only the 42nd person to hold the office. Grover Cleveland, who served two non-consecutive terms (1885–89 and 1893–97) is listed as both the 22nd and 24th president. Table 3.3 shows that of George W. Bush's 41 predecessors, just 11 have served two consecutive full terms. Should he therefore see his current term through to 20 January 2009, George W. Bush will join a very exclusive group of US presidents.

President	Dates	Party
George Washington	1789–97	Federalist
Thomas Jefferson	1801–09	Democratic–Republican
James Madison	1809–17	Democratic–Republican
James Munroe	1817–25	Democratic–Republican
Andrew Jackson	1829–37	Democrat
Ulysses Grant	1869–77	Republican
Woodrow Wilson	1913–21	Democrat
Franklin Roosevelt	1933–45	Democrat
Dwight Eisenhower	1953–61	Republican
Ronald Reagan	1981–89	Republican
Bill Clinton	1993–2001	Democrat

Table 3.3 Presidents who served two full consecutive terms

Bush is already a member of another select group — presidents who were re-elected to office. As well as the 11 named above, a further 7 were re-elected to office but either their first or second term of office was not a full 4-year term (see Table 3.4). Lincoln, McKinley and Nixon were elected to office and then re-elected, but failed to complete their second term. Theodore Roosevelt, Coolidge, Truman and Johnson all succeeded to the presidency following the death of their predecessor and so did not serve a full 4-year first term. They were each elected to office only once.

President	Elected	Re-elected	Reason why two full terms not served
Abraham Lincoln	1860	1864	Assassinated 1865
William McKinley	1896	1900	Assassinated 1901
Theodore Roosevelt	–	1904	Succeeded to presidency
Calvin Coolidge	–	1924	Succeeded to presidency
Harry Truman	–	1948	Succeeded to presidency
Lyndon Johnson	–	1964	Succeeded to presidency
Richard Nixon	1968	1972	Resigned 1974

Table 3.4 Presidents who were re-elected but did not serve two full terms

Although re-election to office is no guarantee of greatness — Calvin Coolidge, Richard Nixon and Bill Clinton, please note — one-term presidents are always regarded as something of a failure. After all, the voters' only verdict on their presidency was to end it. Recent examples of Gerald Ford, Jimmy Carter and George Bush clearly illustrate this point. Thus 20 January 2001 was not just the first day of Bush's first term; it was in many ways also the first day of his re-election campaign. Everything that occurred during those first 4 years must to some extent be seen in that context.

A detailed analysis of why George W. Bush won re-election in 2004 has already appeared in the 2005 edition of this book. Just one further observation may be made here. In 2000, George W. Bush had managed to win an election against the incumbent vice-president at a time of peace and prosperity. It was an election that clearly Vice-President Gore should have won. In 2004, George W. Bush managed to win re-election with a pretty awful economy and poor approval ratings. It was an election that clearly the President should have lost.

In 1980, Republican presidential candidate Ronald Reagan had famously posed the question: 'Are you better off than you were 4 years ago?' The overwhelming answer of 'no' had led to making Jimmy Carter a one-term president. In the 4 years of Bush's first term, the Dow Jones index was down by over 4.4%. The NASDAQ was down a whopping 23.3%. The $236 billion budget surplus on the last day of Bill Clinton's presidency became a projected deficit of some $400 billion. Bush was the only post-Second World War president to have presided over a net decrease in jobs in the USA. That President Bush won a second term against this economic news was certainly remarkable.

Conclusion

Which recent president does George W. Bush most closely resemble? Well, he's certainly not a Bill Clinton. He has none of Mr Clinton's liking for policy detail, oratorical skill or moral indiscipline. The closest match I could suggest is a cross between Ronald Reagan and Lyndon Johnson. Like President Reagan, he's a conservative, he's an ex-governor of a large state, he prefers the big picture to policy detail, and he's frequently underestimated and ridiculed. Opponents find it hard to take him seriously, but they often come away having lost out to him.

However, he also has fellow-Texan Lyndon Johnson's penchant for big government spending and, some would suggest, foreign adventurism. Back in the 1960s and 1970s, one used to talk of Democrat politicians such as Hubert Humphrey and Walter Mondale as 'big government, tax and spend liberals'. George W. Bush is that most odd creature — a big government, tax-cutting conservative! Bill Clinton famously announced in 1996 that 'the era of big government is over'. Under George W. Bush, the era of big government is back. But since when has big government been a *conservative* agenda item?

Ronald Reagan called the Soviet Union 'the evil empire'. George W. Bush has his 'axis of evil'. Reagan once quipped that the most alarming statement in the English language is 'I'm from the federal government and I'm here to help you!' He constantly reminded audiences that the federal government did not create the states, but the states created the federal government. With Reagan the presumption was that if you had a problem, the federal government was likely to screw things up. But George W. Bush has hugely expanded the role and size of the federal government — and not just as regards homeland security, but in areas such as education and faith-based programmes. Whether this is a coherent conservative philosophy is an interesting question. Whether it will outlive a George W. Bush presidency is doubtful.

President Bush's legacy will largely depend on the success — or otherwise — of the campaign in Iraq and the 'war on terror'. If the Clinton years were encapsulated in a finger-wagging President protesting that 'I did not have sexual relations with that woman — Ms Lewinsky', then the George W. Bush presidency will surely be defined by 9/11 and all that stemmed from it. If Mr Bush steps down on 20 January 2009 able to claim that the world in general and the USA in particular is a safer place because of his policies, then shares in George W. Bush will appreciate. Should there be more bloody scenes in US cities and/or the situation in Iraq remains volatile, Mr Bush may become an even rarer political animal — a two-term failure. It's way too early to say yet.

Exercises

1. Which five key dates and events are suggested as the memorable dates of George W. Bush's first term?
2. What disadvantages and difficulties faced George W. Bush during the first months of his presidency – until 11 September 2001?
3. How did Bush handle relations with Congress in these early months?
4. What problems did President Bush face in trying to get in touch with members of his administration on the morning of 11 September 2001?
5. What were the immediate political consequences of 9/11 for the Bush administration?
6. What happened in the 2002 mid-term elections?
7. Discuss George W. Bush's failure to use the veto power during his first term.
8. What problems did President Bush face in getting his judicial nominees confirmed by the Senate during his first term?
9. How did President Bush's support score in Congress during his first term compare with those of his predecessors?
10. How unusual is it for the US president to serve two full terms?
11. Which recent US presidents does the author suggest that President George W. Bush most resembles politically? What reasons are given for this?

Chapter 4

Looking back to 2004 and forward to 2006

Looking back to 2004

The previous edition of this book included a comprehensive analysis of the 2004 presidential election. But during the past year, some more interesting data have become available, including the publication of the presidential election result by congressional district. This allows us to make some observations that are impossible with only the state-by-state results to hand.

Remember that in terms of the popular vote, Bush beat Kerry by 51% to 48%. In the Electoral College, the margin was 286–252. But the latest data show that, of the nation's 435 congressional districts, Bush won 256 to Kerry's 179. Of the 256 congressional districts that were won by George W. Bush, the President out-polled the Republican House of Representatives candidate in only 34 of them — 11 of which were in Bush's home state of Texas. What this shows is a total absence of any **coat-tails effect** in these elections.

> **Key words**
>
> **coat-tails effect:** the effect of a strong candidate for a party at the top of the ticket helping other candidates of the same party to get elected at the same time.
>
> **split-ticket voting:** voting for candidates of two or more parties for different offices in the same election.

Another phenomenon that was hard to find in 2004 was **split-ticket voting**. Only 57 of the 435 congressional districts voted for the candidates of different parties in the presidential and congressional elections. There were 40 congressional districts that voted for George W. Bush for president but voted for a Democrat House member. There were 17 congressional districts that voted for John Kerry for president but voted for a Republican House member.

The data also show how similar the 2004 election was to 2000. We know that only three states — New Mexico, New Hampshire and Iowa — switched party from 2000 to 2004. New Mexico and Iowa switched from Democrat to Republican, while New Hampshire switched from Republican to Democrat. Of the 435 congressional districts, 418 voted the same way in both elections. Only 17 switched: 16 Gore districts from 2000 voted for Bush in 2004 and just 1 Bush district from 2000 voted for Kerry in 2004 — the 4th District of Oregon.

There were 239 congressional districts that voted for George W. Bush in both 2000 and 2004. The percentage of the vote for Bush decreased in only 26 of those districts, which shows that Bush's increase in the vote occurred right across the country, not just in the so-called red states. On the other hand, of the 179 congressional districts that voted for Gore in 2000 and Kerry in 2004, Kerry's vote was lower than Gore's vote in 68 districts. Tables 4.1 and 4.2 show where Bush and Kerry had the largest increase in their vote from 2000 to 2004. Bush's big increases were in a wide range of districts — from Alabama in the south, to New Jersey in the northeast, to California in the west. Kerry's big increases occurred almost exclusively in blue states and mostly in California. The vote for Kerry also fell by a staggering 12 percentage points in New York's 9th District.

Increase in vote from 2000 to 2004 (%)	Congressional district
11	Tennessee 6
10	Alabama 4
8	New Jersey 4
7	Tennessee 1, Tennessee 7
6	Alabama 5, California 41, California 47, Illinois 19, Missouri 4, New Jersey 2, New Jersey 3, Oklahoma 3, Oklahoma 4, Tennessee 2, Texas 10, Utah 1

Table 4.1 Congressional districts showing largest increases in Republican vote, 2000–04

Increase in vote from 2000 to 2004 (%)	Congressional district
8	California 1, California 6, Massachusetts 8, Minnesota 5
7	California 8, California 9, Massachusetts 1, Washington 7
6	California 14, California 17, Virginia 8

Table 4.2 Congressional districts showing largest increases in Democratic vote, 2000–04

Congressional Quarterly also published data that divided congressional districts into four different categories: urban, rural, suburban and mixed (see Table 4.3). What these data suggest is that the part of the USA which most closely reflected the nation as a whole in the 2004 election was the suburban USA. The 51–48% popular vote in suburban districts exactly mirrored the election result nationwide. Over half of the nation's congressional districts (220 out of 435) are in the 'suburban' category.

Type of congressional district	Republican vote (%)	Democratic vote (%)
Urban (90)	38	61
Rural (61)	54	43
Suburban (220)	51	48
Mixed (64)	57	42

Note: figures in brackets indicate the number of districts in each category.

Table 4.3 Vote in 2004 by type of congressional district

Finally, we can use these data to discover what would have been the result of the 2004 presidential election had all 50 states used the system of Electoral

College voting that is used in Maine and Nebraska. In these two states, the Electoral College votes are awarded not on a winner-takes-all basis but to the winner of each congressional district. The remaining two Electoral College votes in each state are awarded to the candidate who wins in the state-wide poll. Under this so-called Maine system, Bush would have increased his Electoral College vote margin over Kerry from 286–252 to 316–222. This would clearly have distorted the nationwide popular vote margin to a greater extent. In fact, the winner-takes-all result of 286–252 almost exactly mirrored the popular vote of 51–48%.

Looking forward to 2006

November 2006 will see the next round of congressional elections. These are what are referred to as 'mid-term elections', as they occur midway through the president's 4-year term of office. All 435 members of the House of Representatives and one-third of the 100-member Senate will be up for re-election. In the last set of mid-term elections in 2002, the Republicans did very well indeed; the more so as it is usual for the president's party to lose seats in both houses of Congress at mid-term elections. But in 2002, George W. Bush's Republicans gained 5 seats in the House of Representatives and 2 in the Senate. This was the first time since 1934 that the president's party had gained seats in both houses at the mid-term elections — no mean achievement.

Since the Senate was directly elected back in 1914, the president's party has lost an average of 31 House seats and 4 Senate seats at the mid-term elections. It is sometimes claimed that the biggest losses tend to occur in those mid-term elections that are held 2 years into a president's second term of office, or, to put it another way, 6 years into a presidency. But the statistics don't entirely support this idea. Table 4.4 shows the losses by the president's party in these second term mid-term elections.

			Gains/losses for president's party in:	
Year	President	Party	House	Senate
1918	Wilson	Democratic	–19	–6
1926	Harding/Coolidge	Republican	–10	–6
1938	Roosevelt	Democratic	–71	–6
1950	Roosevelt/Truman	Democratic	–29	–6
1958	Eisenhower	Republican	–48	–13
1966	Kennedy/Johnson	Democratic	–47	–4
1974	Nixon/Ford	Republican	–48	–5
1986	Reagan	Republican	–5	–8
1998	Clinton	Democratic	+5	0

Table 4.4 Gains and losses by the president's party in second-term mid-term elections, 1918–98

The average loss for the president's party in these elections is 30 House seats — almost identical with the overall figure of 31 — and 6 Senate seats. Table 4.4 also shows that in both 1986 and 1998 — 6 years respectively into the Reagan and Clinton presidencies — no such cataclysmic loss occurred at all. Indeed, in 1998, at the height of the Clinton impeachment drama, the Democrats managed to gain 5 House seats and maintain the status quo in the Senate. On this basis, therefore, the Democrats might be foolish to start counting their chickens.

In 2004, only 30 of the 435 seats in the House of Representatives were won with less than 55% of the vote. Of these 30 seats, 18 are held by the Republicans and 12 by the Democrats. The Republicans currently hold an effective 29-seat majority in the House. This means that the Democrats need to make an overall gain of 15 House seats to become the majority party. While this is well within the average for mid-term elections, it would mean the Democrats having to win over 80% of these vulnerable Republican seats while holding all of their own. That sounds a rather tougher proposition.

In the Senate, the 33 seats being contested in 2006 are the ones that were last contested in 2000. Of these, 17 are currently held by the Democrats, 15 by the Republicans and the other by the independent (and former Republican) James Jeffords. Only 9 of these 33 seats were won with less than 55% of the popular vote last time around, thereby putting them into the 'vulnerable' category. And as Table 4.5 shows, of those 9 potentially vulnerable seats, 5 are held by Democrats and only 4 by Republicans. The Republicans currently hold an effective 10-seat majority in the Senate. This means that the Democrats need to make an overall gain of 6 Senate seats to become the majority party. As we have just seen, this is exactly the average of second-term mid-term election losses by the president's party. But it means that the Democrats have to hold all of their 5 most vulnerable seats, win all the 4 Republican vulnerable seats, plus 2 more. Again, that could be quite difficult to achieve.

Senator	State	Party	Percentage of vote in 2000
Debbie Stabenow	Michigan	Democratic	49
Mark Dayton	Minnesota	Democratic	49
Maria Cantwell	Washington	Democratic	49
Jim Talent*	Missouri	Republican	50
Conrad Burns	Montana	Republican	50
Bill Nelson	Florida	Democratic	51
Ben Nelson	Nebraska	Democratic	51
Rick Santorum	Pennsylvania	Republican	52
George Allen	Virginia	Republican	52

*Jim Talent was elected in 2002 to complete the term to which Mel Carnahan was elected in 2000, but who died before the election was held.

Table 4.5 Senators who won with less than 55% of the vote in the previous election

There are three open seats, caused by the retirement of the incumbent senator. Democrat Paul Sarbanes of Maryland has announced that he will not run again. Republican Bill Frist of Tennessee has announced that he will not run. He is believed to be planning a presidential bid for 2008. The third open seat is the one currently held by James Jeffords of Vermont, who is retiring. Jeffords was re-elected with 66% of the vote as a Republican in 2000. But within 6 months of taking his seat, he left the Republican Party and has since sat as an independent. Jeffords usually votes with the Democrats and therefore this should be considered as a Democrat-held seat.

Open seats usually offer the best chances for the opposition to make gains. But it seems possible that all three of these open seats will remain with the party that currently holds them. The seven seemingly most vulnerable senators are Republicans Rick Santorum (Pennsylvania) and Jim Talent (Missouri) along with Democrats Bill Nelson (Florida), Ben Nelson (Nebraska), Debbie Stabenow (Michigan), Mark Dayton (Minnesota) and Maria Cantwell (Washington).

Looking at the Senate races from the red state/blue state perspective, there are 5 Democrat-held seats being defended in red states, and there are 3 Republican-held seats being defended in blue states. But only three of these races look potentially interesting — those in Florida, Nebraska and Pennsylvania.

The one wild card in all this must be the condition of the Bush presidency in general, and maybe of Iraq and the 'war on terror' in particular, when election day comes around on Tuesday 7 November. Mid-term elections are often a barometer of the state of the presidency, as Bill Clinton found out to his cost in 1994 and George W. Bush found out to his benefit in 2002. In the 1994 mid-term elections, Clinton's Democrats lost 52 House seats and 8 Senate seats. In 2002, George W. Bush's Republicans gained 5 House seats and 2 Senate seats. Watch those presidential approval numbers through 2006. They could hold the key to the outcome.

Exercises

1 What is the 'coat-tails effect'? What evidence is there that President George W. Bush enjoyed no coat-tails effect in the 2004 elections?

2 What is split-ticket voting? What evidence is there that there was very little ticket-splitting in the 2004 elections?

3 What is the Maine system of allocating Electoral College votes in the presidential election? What would have been the result of the 2004 presidential election had all 50 states used this system?

4 What tends to happen to the president's party in mid-term elections?

5 Why is it less likely that the president's party will suffer heavy losses in the Senate and the House in the 2006 mid-term congressional elections?

Chapter 5

The Supreme Court, 2004–05

What you need to know

- The Supreme Court is the highest federal court in the USA.
- Supreme Court justices are appointed by the president and confirmed by the Senate.
- They are appointed for life.
- There are nine justices on the Supreme Court: one Chief Justice and eight associate justices.
- Of the current nine justices, seven have been appointed by Republican presidents and only two by Democrats.
- The Supreme Court has the power of judicial review. This is the power to declare acts of Congress or actions of the executive branch — or acts or actions of state governments — unconstitutional, and thereby null and void.
- By this power of judicial review, the Court acts as the umpire of the Constitution and plays a leading role in guaranteeing Americans' rights and liberties.

The final term with the same justices

The Supreme Court gathered for its new term in October 2004 with the same nine justices for the eleventh consecutive, but last, year. Not since Justice Stephen Breyer joined the Court back in 1994 had there been any change in its membership. In the previous 11 years (1983–94), six new justices had joined the Court and Rehnquist had been elevated to the post of Chief Justice. On average, a Supreme Court vacancy occurs every 2 years. The longest period of stability in Supreme Court membership in the Court's 216-year history remains the 12-year period between Gabriel Duvall joining the Court in 1811 and Smith Thompson joining in 1823. The 11-year period between 1994 and 2005 ranks as the second longest. The ages of the nine justices and their length of service at the close of their 2004–05 term are shown in Table 5.1. The average age of the Court was then (June 2005) just over 71 and the average length of service just short of 20 years. Between them, the nine justices had by then totalled 173 years of service on the Supreme Court!

Justice	Age at the end of 2004–05 term (years/months)	Length of service at the end of 2004–05 term (years/months)
William Rehnquist	80.9	33.6
John Paul Stevens	85.2	29.6
Sandra Day O'Connor	75.3	23.9
Antonin Scalia	69.3	18.9
Anthony Kennedy	69.0	16.4
David Souter	65.9	14.8
Clarence Thomas	57.0	13.8
Ruth Bader Ginsburg	72.3	11.10
Stephen Breyer	66.10	10.11

Table 5.1 Age and length of service of Supreme Court justices, June 2005

There is also evidence that the character of the Supreme Court has changed during recent decades. From 1789 to 1970, the average Supreme Court justice served for 15 years and retired at 68 years of age. But since 1970, the average tenure for a Supreme Court justice has risen significantly to over 25 years and the average retirement age during these years has been just short of 79.

This degree of stability has been important. In an institution as small as the nine-member Supreme Court, the interaction between the justices can be significantly altered by just one change of membership. After working together for 11 years, these justices built up an unusually high level of understanding of the philosophy of their colleagues. New justices bring new perspectives, reflecting perhaps the philosophy of US society at the time of their recruitment. In this sense, the 2004–05 Court can be thought of as something of an 'echo chamber' — echoing times past from the 1970s, 1980s and 1990s, when the justices were recruited to the Court. US society has moved on a good deal since the days when Chief Justice William Rehnquist or Associate Justice John Paul Stevens joined the Court, some 30 years ago. Even Stephen Breyer, the most recent recruit, had joined in 1994, over 7 years before the events of 11 September 2001.

The 2004–05 term

Some Supreme Court terms will go down in history as landmark events, for during them the Court has delivered a judgement of such historic importance that it will be remembered for decades — maybe centuries — to come. Like its immediate predecessor, 2004–05 was not such a term. Nonetheless, nine selected cases are considered below (see Table 5.2). Three of these were of particular importance. In these three cases — as in a number of others — the Court was revisiting policy areas into which it had delved in previous terms: freedom of religion and the death penalty.

Case	Concerning	Decided by
McCreary County, Kentucky v. *ACLU*	Freedom of religion	5–4
Van Orden v. *Perry*	Freedom of religion	5–4
Roper v. *Simmons*	Death penalty	5–4
Illinois v. *Caballes*	Unreasonable searches	6–2
Kelo v. *City of New London*	Property rights	5–4
Miller-El v. *Dretke*	Right to a fair trial	6–3
Halbert v. *Michigan*	Right to legal representation	6–3
Town of Castle Rock v. *Gonzales*	Due process	7–2
Gonzales v. *Raich*	Federal–state powers	6–3

Table 5.2 Important Supreme Court decisions, 2004–05 term

Freedom of religion

Two of the most important cases of this term were delivered by the Court on its final day. These were two cases dealing with the vexed question of freedom of religion and what is known as the separation of church and state. The 1st Amendment, added to the Constitution in 1791, begins with the following words:

> Congress shall make no law respecting the establishment of religion, or prohibiting the free exercise thereof.

The **Founding Fathers** believed that it was vitally important to prevent the government from establishing a religion. Many of their forebears had fled religious persecution in Europe and they did not wish to resurrect the days when they might again fall foul of the 'established' religion. Equally, they believed that Americans should be free to practise their religion. Hence the two, potentially conflicting, parts of the opening sentence of the First Amendment. It was never going to be easy to ensure that both these provisions were kept. Critics of the Supreme Court would say that, for the last four decades, the Court has been much more interested in ensuring that there is 'no law respecting the establishment of religion' than in protecting its 'free exercise'.

Key word

Founding Fathers: those who wrote the new federal Constitution at the Philadelphia Convention in the summer of 1787 and thereby founded the United States of America.

In 2005, the Court had two cases before it that seemed very similar. In the case of *McCreary County, Kentucky* v. *American Civil Liberties Union*, the Court was being asked whether or not framed copies of the Ten Commandments on the walls of two Kentucky courthouses were a breach of the First Amendment protection against 'the establishment of religion'. In the case of *Van Orden* v. *Perry*, the Court was being asked whether a 6-foot-tall granite monument bearing the Ten Commandments was constitutional.

Given the similarity of the cases, one might have expected the Court to have decided either that both were, or that both were not, constitutional. But the Court managed to arrive at different decisions in these two cases, deciding that whereas the framed courthouse copies must be removed, the granite monument can live on.

The framed copies of the Ten Commandments appeared in the Kentucky courthouses in the summer of 1999. The Kentucky branch of the American Civil Liberties Union (ACLU), a well-known liberal interest group, challenged their appearance. The Kentucky state authorities replied by passing resolutions calling the commandments the 'precedent legal code' for Kentucky's laws. They also added other items with a religious theme, such as Abraham Lincoln's declaration of a national day of prayer in 1863. After a federal judge ordered the Ten Commandments to be removed in 2000, the authorities merely added some secular exhibits such as a copy of Magna Carta and the lyrics of 'The Star-Spangled Banner'. In a 5–4 decision, the Supreme Court agreed with ACLU that displaying the Ten Commandments ran contrary to the provisions of the First Amendment. In his majority opinion, Justice David Souter stated that the addition of the secular items could not disguise the county's true purpose, which was 'to emphasise and celebrate the Commandments' religious message.' The dissenting justices were three conservatives — William Rehnquist, Antonin Scalia and Clarence Thomas — joined by Anthony Kennedy.

On the other hand, the granite monument in Austin, Texas, which was the subject of the related case, had been placed there in 1961. And for over 40 years, not a single objection to it was raised. It is also only one of 38 such items situated within the 22-acre grounds of the Texas state capitol. But in 2002, Thomas Van Orden, a homeless man — and former law student — claimed he was offended by this particular edifice. In a 5–4 decision, the Supreme Court disagreed with Mr Van Orden. The dissenting judges in this case were three liberals — John Paul Stevens, David Souter and Ruth Bader Ginsburg — joined by Sandra Day O'Connor.

Justice Stephen Breyer — the only justice to be in the majority on both opinions — wrote in the Texas case:

> This [Texas] display has stood apparently uncontested for nearly two generations. That experience helps us understand that as a practical matter of *degree* this display is unlikely to prove divisive.

But then, in a reference to the Kentucky case, he added:

> In a nation of so many different religious and comparable nonreligious fundamental beliefs, a more contemporary state effort to focus attention upon a religious text is certainly likely to prove divisive in a way that this longstanding, pre-existing monument has not.

Justice Antonin Scalia, one of the four dissenters in the Kentucky decision, said the decision was inconsistent with the Founding Fathers' views and 'ratchets up this Court's hostility to religion'.

The decisions seem to generate more heat than light. 'Our frustration is, it's very difficult to tell what kind of display would be constitutional,' complained the Mayor of Boise, Idaho, where a similar debate is going on. Context seems to be the key. The Texas Commandments were acceptable, as they were always part of a larger display. The Kentucky Commandments, on the other hand, were put up to draw attention to the religious faith with which they are associated. Kentuckians might be envious of the Texans' good fortune. But then they might be breaking the tenth commandment!

Death penalty

The **8th Amendment** to the Constitution forbids 'cruel or unusual [arbitrary or unfair] punishments'. Over the past three decades, the Court has made a number of rulings on the way in which the death penalty does or does not infringe this constitutional provision. Most of the decisions have nibbled away at the death penalty. Three years ago, we considered the 2002 decision in *Atkins* v. *Virginia* (see *US Government & Politics Annual Survey 2003*, pp. 37–40), in which the Supreme Court declared the execution of mentally retarded citizens to be unconstitutional.

> **8th Amendment (1791)**
>
> 'Excessive bail shall not be required, nor excessive fines imposed, nor cruel and unusual punishments inflicted.'

In 2005, the Court had more to say on the subject of the death penalty in *Roper* v. *Simmons*, in which the Court declared that it is unconstitutional — a violation of the 8th Amendment — to sentence anyone to death for a crime that he or she committed when younger than 18 years of age. The case arose after 17-year-old Christopher Simmons broke into a house in Missouri in September 1993 and kidnapped the owner — Shirley Crook — before throwing her, bound and gagged, into a river.

> **Key word**
>
> **strict constructionist:** describes the view that judges should interpret the Constitution in a strict, literal or conservative fashion; that judges should not 'make law', but should leave that to the legislature.

This was the third of the most important decisions handed down by the Supreme Court in this term. And, like the other two, it was a 5–4 decision, the dissenting justices this time being the four most conservative members of the Court — Rehnquist, O'Connor, Scalia and Thomas. O'Connor actually agreed with the idea that those who had committed crimes under the age of 18 should not be subject to the death penalty, but true to her **strict constructionist** views, she stated that this was for the legislature to sort out, not the judiciary. Indeed, O'Connor even stated in her minority opinion that, were she a legislator, 'I, too, would be inclined to support legislation setting a minimum age of 18 in this context.'

In *Stanford* v. *Kentucky* (1989) the Court had ruled — again by 5–4 — that 16 should be the minimum age for the death penalty. Of the five justices who remained from the time of that decision, four remained consistent in their views. Rehnquist, O'Connor and Scalia all supported the Stanford decision and now opposed the Roper decision, while Stevens, who had opposed the Stanford decision, was now in the majority in Roper. The only switcher was Anthony Kennedy — often referred to as the 'swing justice' — who was in favour of setting the limit at 16 in 1989 but now opposed it 16 years later, thereby causing the Court to reverse its 1989 decision.

Back in 1989 when the Court had last ruled on the age-related issue of the death penalty, 25 states permitted the death penalty for offenders younger than 18. By 2005, this number had declined to 20, including Virginia from which state the Roper case originated. And as Figure 5.1 shows, the year in which the case was heard by the Supreme Court (2004) saw the fewest executions in the USA since 1996.

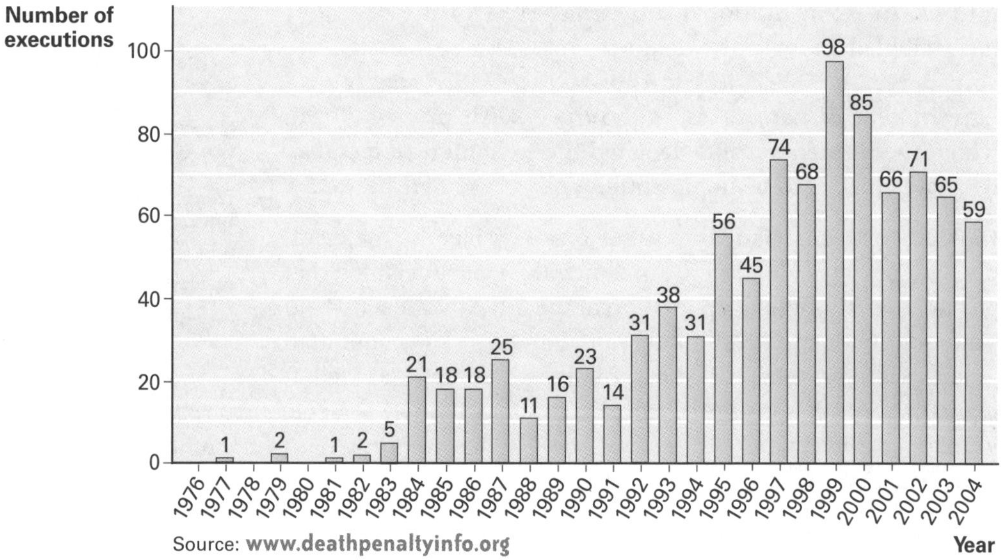

Figure 5.1 Executions in the USA, 1976–2004

Writing for the majority, Justice Anthony Kennedy stated:

> Retribution is not proportional if the law's most severe penalty is imposed on one whose culpability or blameworthiness is diminished, to a substantial degree, by reason of youth or immaturity.

The Court's liberal majority argued that their decision also sat well with society's ongoing reconsideration of the death penalty debate, not only in the USA but elsewhere in western democracies, even quoting approvingly from the European Union's statements against the death penalty. Anthony Kennedy, for example, stated that the strong expression of international opinion against the death penalty 'provides respected and significant confirmation for our own conclusions'.

This was all too much for conservative justice Antonin Scalia, who criticised the majority for trying to proclaim themselves as 'the sole arbiter of our Nation's moral standards — and in the course of discharging that awesome responsibility, purporting to take guidance from the views of foreign courts and legislatures'. He accused the Court of 'invoking alien law when it agrees with one's own thinking and ignoring it otherwise'. In case that wasn't clear enough, Scalia concluded:

> I do not believe that the meaning of our 8th Amendment should be determined by the subjective views of five members of this Court and like-minded foreigners. The views of our own citizens are essentially irrelevant. Instead we give centre stage to the so-called international community.

Other Bill of Rights cases

The Court handed down three other judgements relating to the **Bill of Rights** that are worthy of note. In *Illinois* v. *Caballes* the Court decided (6–2: Chief Justice Rehnquist did not offer an opinion) that an Illinois state trooper's search of a car for drugs after having pulled over the driver for a speeding offence did not constitute an 'unreasonable search', which is forbidden by the **4th Amendment**. The two dissenting justices in this case were liberals David Souter and Ruth Bader Ginsburg.

Key word

Bill of Rights: the first ten amendments, added to the Constitution in 1791, in order to protect fundamental rights and liberties.

4th Amendment (1791)
'The right of the people to be secure in their persons, houses, papers, and effects, against unreasonable searches and seizures, shall not be violated.'

5th Amendment (1791)
'No persons shall be... deprived of life, liberty or property, without due process of law.'

6th Amendment (1791)
'In all criminal prosecutions, the accused shall enjoy the right to a speedy and public trial by an impartial jury of the State and district wherein the crime shall have been committed.'

In *Kelo* v. *City of New London*, the Court decided that local governments may force property owners to sell in order to make way for private economic development without infringing the property rights provision of the **5th Amendment**. In a 5–4 decision, the dissenters were the four conservative justices — Rehnquist, O'Connor, Scalia and Thomas.

And in *Miller-El* v. *Dretke*, the Court ordered the state of Texas to grant a new trial to a black death row inmate, who alleged that state prosecutors had stacked his jury with white people and thereby infringed his **6th Amendment** rights to a fair trial. Rehnquist, Scalia and Thomas yet again dissented in this 6–3 decision.

14th Amendment cases

The Court handed down two decisions relating to the 'equal protection' and 'due process' clauses of the 14th Amendment. In *Halbert* v. *Michigan*, the

Court struck down a Michigan state law as unconstitutional because it infringed the 14th Amendment rights to legal representation. Antonio Halbert had pleaded guilty in 2001 to child molestation charges. When he was sentenced to 30 years in jail he wanted a state-appointed lawyer to help him appeal the sentence. But Michigan had passed a law in 1994 barring anyone who appealed following a 'guilty' plea from receiving state-paid legal aid. In a 6–3 decision, the Court ruled that this law infringed a fundamental civil right. Writing for the majority, Ruth Bader Ginsburg stated:

> Navigating the appellate process without a lawyer's assistance is a perilous endeavour for a layperson, and well beyond the competence of individuals, like Halbert, who have little education, learning disabilities, and mental impairments.

Michigan had passed the law to clear a backlog of thousands of appeal cases. Seventeen other states had passed similar legislation. Yet again, Rehnquist, Scalia and Thomas dissented.

In *Town of Castle Rock* v. *Gonzales*, the Court ruled that police cannot be sued for how they enforce restraining orders. Jessica Gonzales of Castle Rock, Colorado, had sought to hold state police responsible for failing to enforce a restraining order against her estranged husband, who then killed her three daughters before being fatally shot by police. The decision (by 7–2 with Stevens and Ginsburg dissenting) was seen as a victory for states and cities who feared costly lawsuits if Gonzales's claim had been upheld.

Compassionate use of marijuana

Finally, a case that generated much interest revolved around California's Compassionate Use Act. In *Gonzales* v. *Raich*, the Court upheld the power of Congress to prohibit the possession and use of marijuana for medical purposes, even in the 11 states that permit it. The decision was seen as a strong affirmation of federal government power over that of state governments. In the 6–3 decision, Justice Stevens writing for the majority stated that the federal government had the power 'to regulate commerce' through Article I of the Constitution. Battles over the federal–state balance have been a common feature of the Supreme Court in recent years. Most have been won by the conservative majority upholding states' rights over federal government power. But this time, the conservative camp was deserted by Justices Scalia and Kennedy, leaving Rehnquist, O'Connor and Thomas in a minority.

Court statistics

In the 2004–05 term, the Supreme Court delivered 74 full opinions, compared with 73 in the previous term. Of these, 22 (30%) were decided by a margin of 5–4, compared with 25% the previous term (see Table 5.3). The justice most frequently in the majority in 2004–05 was Clinton appointee Stephen Breyer. For the 7 previous years, that distinction had gone to Justice Sandra Day

O'Connor, shared with Chief Justice Rehnquist in 2001–02. Breyer cast only 10 dissenting votes during the term; O'Connor cast 11.

	2000–01	2001–02	2002–03	2003–04	2004–05
Number of cases	77	79	71	73	74
Decided by 5–4	32%	27%	20%	25%	30%
Most frequently in majority	O'Connor	O'Connor/ Rehnquist	O'Connor	O'Connor	Breyer

Table 5.3 Supreme Court statistics, 2000–05

This clearly indicates that the Court has continued its move to the centre — an extraordinary fact given that only 2 of its members have been appointed by Democratic presidents. In the 9 most important decisions of the 2004–05 term, Justice Breyer was in the majority in all 9 cases, while the 3 most conservative justices — Rehnquist, Scalia and Thomas — could muster only 9 majority opinions between them (see Table 5.4).

	Stevens	Ginsburg	Souter	Breyer	O'Connor	Kennedy	Rehnquist	Scalia	Thomas
McCreary	Yes	Yes	Yes	Yes	Yes	No	No	No	No
Van Orden	No	No	No	Yes	No	Yes	Yes	Yes	Yes
Roper	Yes	Yes	Yes	Yes	No	Yes	No	No	No
Illinois	Yes	No	No	Yes	Yes	Yes	–	Yes	Yes
Kelo	Yes	Yes	Yes	Yes	No	Yes	No	No	No
Miller-El	Yes	Yes	Yes	Yes	Yes	Yes	No	No	No
Halbert	Yes	Yes	Yes	Yes	Yes	Yes	No	No	No
Castle Rock	No	No	Yes	Yes	Yes	Yes	Yes	Yes	Yes
Gonzales	Yes	Yes	Yes	Yes	No	Yes	No	Yes	No
Total cases in majority (out of 9)	**7**	**6**	**7**	**9**	**5**	**8**	**2**	**4**	**3**

Table 5.4 Majority opinions in important decisions, 2004–05 term

Another trend that was discernible during 2004–05 was the fracturing of what one might call the 'conservative coalition' on the Court. In 2003–04, for example, the 5 most conservative members of the Court — Rehnquist, Scalia, Thomas, Kennedy and O'Connor — voted together in half of the 18 5–4 decisions. But in this term, the same 5 voted together in only 4 (18%) of the 22 decisions that were decided by 5 votes to 4.

It is easy to over-generalise when speaking of the justices of the Supreme Court. Justices Breyer and Ginsburg — the 2 Clinton appointees — are, for example, seen as being the same in terms of judicial philosophy. Yet of this term's 48 split decisions, Ginsburg and Breyer were on opposite sides in 11 cases (24%). The same goes for Scalia and Thomas, who are often portrayed as the conservative identical twins of the Court. But they found themselves on opposite sides in 12 (25%) of the term's 48 split decisions.

The 2005–06 Court will have a different make-up, so changes will come both from outside and maybe still from within the Court. New alliances will be formed. The term will be a particularly interesting one to watch.

Exercises

1 What was (a) the average age, (b) the average length of service and (c) the combined total years of service of the Supreme Court justices during the 2004–05 term?

2 Explain the decisions that the Supreme Court made in 2004–05 over the display of the Ten Commandments in public places. Why did the Court uphold the display in one case but strike it down in the other?

3 How did the decision in *Roper* v. *Simmons* extend the Court's ruling on the death penalty?

4 What does Figure 5.1 show about the number of executions performed in the USA since 1976?

5 What did the Court have to say about 4th, 5th and 6th Amendment rights during the 2004–05 term?

6 What was the significance of the Court's decision in the case of *Gonzales* v. *Raich*?

7 Which judge was most frequently in the majority during the 2004–05 term? Why is this somewhat surprising?

8 What does Table 5.4 tell us about the decisions in the 9 most important cases decided by the Supreme Court in the 2004–05 term?

Chapter 6

A new chief justice of the United States

What you need to know

- The United States Supreme Court is made up of nine justices: one chief justice and eight associate justices.
- Nominations to the Court are made by the president with the advice and consent of the Senate.
- Appointments to the Court are for life.
- Hence the president can make a nomination only upon the death or voluntary retirement of a member of the Court.
- On average, appointments are made approximately every 2 years.
- There were no vacancies on the Court between 1994 and 2005.

No Rehnquist retirement at close of term

So, after 11 years without change, the United States Supreme Court has both a new chief justice and a new associate justice. Although on average vacancies occur approximately every 2 years, there had been no vacancy since 1994 when President Clinton appointed Stephen Breyer to the Supreme Court — the longest period of continuity on the Supreme Court since 1823.

Retirements from the Court are often announced on the last day of the Court's term in late June. The Court concluded its 2004–05 term on Monday 27 June. 'No Retirement Announcements at High Court,' headlined the *Washington Post* in its report on the Court's final day. This was something of a surprise as many commentators and Court watchers had expected Chief Justice William Rehnquist to announce his retirement that day. Rehnquist, an appointee of President Nixon in 1971, was by then 80 years old and suffering from cancer. The *Washington Post* reported:

> The chief justice had difficulty as he announced the final ruling of the term. His breathing was laboured. The atmosphere was tense as spectators leaned forward in their seats trying to hear Rehnquist's closing remarks. Rehnquist, sometimes taking long pauses, announced the October 3rd starting date for the next session and thanked the staff for their outstanding work. He then gavelled the session to a close, stood up slowly and leaned on the back of his leather chair as he turned away from the audience, stepped carefully down a few steps and disappeared behind the Court's massive curtains along with his fellow justices.

Many then presumed that the Supreme Court would begin its 2005–06 term with the same membership as it had begun the last 11 terms. But that was not to be.

O'Connor announces retirement

Four days after the end of the Court's 2004–05 term, Associate Justice Sandra Day O'Connor sent a simple, three-sentence letter to President Bush. Dated 1 July 2005, the letter read:

> This is to inform you of my decision to retire from my position as an Associate Justice of the Supreme Court of the United States effective upon the nomination and confirmation of my successor. It has been a great privilege, indeed, to have served as a member of the Court for 24 terms. I will leave it with enormous respect for the integrity of the Court and its role under our Constitutional structure.

O'Connor was by this time 75 years old and had served on the Supreme Court for 24 years since her appointment by President Reagan in 1981. She was the first woman ever appointed to the Court. Her appointment had also been unusual in that she was recruited not from the federal appeal courts — the normal recruitment pool for Supreme Court justices — but from the Arizona state appeal court.

President Bush, appearing in the White House Rose Garden an hour after receiving the hand-delivered letter, praised O'Connor as 'a discerning and conscientious judge' and promised to nominate a successor 'who will faithfully interpret the Constitution'. The President added:

> The nation deserves and I will select a Supreme Court justice that Americans can be proud of. The nation also deserves a dignified process of confirmation in the United States Senate, characterised by fair treatment, a fair hearing and a fair vote.

These latter comments were oblique references to the stand-off between the Republican President Bush and Senate Democrats over the Senate's treatment of a significant number of the President's lower federal court nominations in recent years. The President then phoned Justice O'Connor and they had what White House staffers described as an emotional conversation. Referring to O'Connor's Arizona background, the President joked: 'For an old ranching girl, you turned out pretty good!' But as events turned out, O'Connor's days on the Supreme Court were not yet over.

The search for a successor

It is always said that a president must wait for a vacancy on the Supreme Court before he can begin the process of nominating a new justice. And although this is strictly true, the events surrounding this vacancy show that a president who anticipates a vacancy may discreetly begin the search for a new justice in advance of the vacancy being announced. Sandra Day O'Connor's resignation was announced on 1 July 2005. But we now know that the Bush White House had begun the search for a new justice 3 months before that. On 1 April 2005 the eventual nominee, John G. Roberts, had his first interview with Attorney General Alberto Gonzales. We discovered this when the White House released documents relating to Roberts's recruitment. Following his April interview with the Attorney General, Roberts then had a second round of interviews on 3 May with Vice-President Dick Cheney and top White House staffers, including Chief of Staff Andrew Card and Deputy Chief of Staff Karl Rove. Roberts was then interviewed by the White House Counsel Harriet Miers on 23 May and again — after O'Connor's announcement — on 8 July. What this reveals is the careful series of interviews conducted by the White House before the nomination was announced. What we don't know, of course, is who else was put through the same process. But it is certain that the White House would have been seriously considering a number of possible nominees.

The announcement that the President was nominating Judge John Roberts to the Supreme Court came just 18 days after the O'Connor resignation letter — on 19 July. Roberts's career path looked much like that of many Supreme Court justices. Born in 1955 in Buffalo, New York, Roberts graduated from Harvard Law School in 1979. The following year found him in Washington as a clerk to Supreme Court Justice William Rehnquist before he moved to the Justice Department as a special assistant to Reagan's Attorney General William French Smith. From there he moved to the White House, spending 4 years as a White House counsel in the Reagan administration. This was followed by 3 years in the prestigious Washington law firm of Hogan and Hartson. Following the first George Bush's election in 1988, Roberts returned to the Justice Department as deputy solicitor general before returning to Hogan and Hartson as a partner in 1993. During those years, Roberts argued 39 cases before the Supreme Court. In 2003, President George W. Bush nominated Roberts to the federal appeals court. The Senate Judiciary Committee approved the nomination by 16 votes to 3 and the Senate confirmed his nomination by voice vote on 8 May of that year. The three 'no' votes in the Senate Judiciary Committee were cast by liberal Democrats Charles Schumer of New York, Richard Durbin of Illinois and Edward Kennedy of Massachusetts. Like eight of the nine members of the Supreme Court with whom he would serve, Roberts was recruited directly from the federal appeals court.

Initial reactions expose Democrat divisions

The initial reaction to the Roberts nomination was certainly pleasing to the White House. Republicans rushed to praise him as a superb jurist. Even leading Democrats were found making comments not exactly hostile to the nominee. The Senate Minority Leader, Harry Reid, noted that Roberts had 'suitable legal credentials' to be a member of the Supreme Court.

Democrats had threatened a blitz of television advertisements against any Supreme Court nominee whom they judged to be outside the mainstream. But when an abortion rights group aired a television advert suggesting that Roberts condoned violence against abortion clinics, the Democratic Party leadership pressured them into pulling the ad off the airwaves. This exposed a division within the Democratic Party that seems to have opened up since the 2002 mid-term elections and the vote to authorise military action in Iraq — a division between the more cautious party leadership in Washington DC and the more militant rank and file membership in the country. In the 2004 presidential election, this division was clearly illustrated in the campaigns of John Kerry and Howard Dean. Kerry represented the more cautious position of the party leadership. He had voted in the Senate in support of the Iraq war. Dean, on the other hand, represented the more militant position of the rank and file, bitterly criticising the President for the Iraq adventure right from the start of the nomination campaign. Simon Rosenberg, co-founder of the New Politics Institute, a think-tank for progressive politics and new technology, summed it up this way:

> Rank-and-file Democrats want the Washington party to fight every day on every issue and to fight more effectively and better. But the truth is, it's going to be hard to fight and win every battle. It's finding that right balance that's going to be the art of keeping the Democratic Party coalition together for the next few years.

The Democratic leadership feared that picking too many fights with Republicans would turn off crucial swing voters both at the mid-term elections in 2006 and in the presidential election in 2008. So all seemed set for Judge Roberts's confirmation hearings to begin in the Senate Judiciary Committee on 6 September when suddenly everything was thrown into confusion.

Chief Justice Rehnquist dies

It was early on the morning of Saturday 3 September that the death of Chief Justice William Rehnquist was announced. Rehnquist was only the sixteenth person to hold the office of chief justice of the United States. His 19 years in the post made him the longest-serving chief justice since Melville Fuller (1888–1910). The announcement of Rehnquist's death came right in the midst of the aftermath of Hurricane Katrina, which had hit the Gulf Coast of Louisiana, Mississippi and Alabama just 5 days earlier. In creating two vacancies on the Court, it threw the selection process for O'Connor's successor into disarray. The hearings on Judge Roberts to fill that vacancy were due to start in the Senate Judiciary Committee in just 3 days time and the opening of the 2005–06 session of the Court was just a month away.

The Bush White House therefore faced something of a difficulty. If Rehnquist's seat was still unfilled on 3 October, the Court would begin its new term with only eight justices on the bench. O'Connor had already announced that she would remain on the Court until her successor had been confirmed by the Senate. President Bush therefore decided on a switch. In a Labor Day press conference at the White House, the President announced that he was now nominating John Roberts as chief justice to replace Rehnquist rather than as an associate justice to replace O'Connor. As the Senate had already begun informal consideration of the Roberts nomination, he hoped that the hearings on Roberts as chief justice could begin almost immediately and therefore be concluded by 3 October. Roberts could then fill Rehnquist's vacancy and O'Connor would probably need to return to the Court for a short period while her successor was confirmed. But the Court would continue to have its full complement of nine justices throughout.

The Roberts confirmation hearings

On Monday 12 September 2005, just 9 days after the death of Chief Justice William Rehnquist, the Senate began its first confirmation hearings on a chief justice for nearly two decades. The hearings began against the background of Hurricane Katrina's devastation of the Gulf Coast states.

In his opening day remarks to the Senate Judiciary Committee, Roberts attempted to allay fears that he was a conservative ideologue in the mould of Robert Bork and to persuade members of the Senate that they could confirm him knowing that he understood well the role of a judge.

> Judges and [Supreme Court] justices are servants of the law. Judges are like umpires. Umpires don't make the rules; they apply them. The role of an umpire and a judge is critical. They make sure everybody plays by the rules. But it is a limited role. Nobody ever went to a ball game to see the umpire. I come before this committee with no agenda. I have no platform. Judges are not politicians who can promise to do certain things in exchange for votes.

It was a shrewd opening pitch. The subtext seemed to be: don't ask me questions about politics, for I'm not a politician. It was all very low key, in direct contrast to the fireworks that had been talked about as the Senate waited for over 11 years for a Supreme Court confirmation hearing. Indeed, at just 7 minutes, Roberts's opening day statement was the shortest anyone could remember. The hearings even failed to make the top news story of the day as the Federal Emergency Management Agency (FEMA) Director Michael Brown resigned mid-morning over the post-Hurricane Katrina shambles. As Dana Milbank commented in the *Washington Post*: 'Roberts may well be confirmed as chief justice of the Supreme Court, but in the case before the court of public attention, in *Katrina* v. *Roberts*, the defendant doesn't have a chance.'

Indeed, the whole confirmation hearing was characterised by the deftness and politeness of the nominee. He was brilliant at turning away questions with answers that gave little away. What did he think of *Roe* v. *Wade*? 'I think I should stay away from discussions of particular issues that are likely to come before the Court again.' What did he think of the war powers of the president and Congress? 'I don't want to answer a particular hypothetical.' What did he think of voting rights? 'Those cases come up all the time, and I do need to avoid expressing an opinion.'

When the committee's questioning turned directly to the matter of abortion and the Supreme Court's precedent-setting case of *Roe* v. *Wade* in 1973, Roberts encouraged Democrat Senator Joseph Biden by saying that the 14th Amendment did protect the right to privacy. But he then immediately qualified that by adding: 'I think every justice on the Court believes that, to some extent or other.' Back in December 1981, as a member of the Reagan Justice Department, Roberts had written a memo on 'the so-called right to privacy'. But when asked during the hearings by Chairman Arlen Specter: 'Do you believe today that the right to privacy does exist in the Constitution?' Roberts replied: 'I do.'

The newspaper columnists were generally impressed with Roberts's performance in front of the Senate Judiciary Committee. According to the *Los Angeles Times*, Roberts 'exuded the quiet confidence of a man who knew he was ahead in the game'. To the *New York Times*, Roberts 'explained his views and defended his honour with the force and fluidity of an advocate who has argued often before tougher judges than those he faced on the Senate Judiciary Committee'.

Committee Democrats were frustrated by Roberts's deftness at avoiding many specifics. New York Democrat Charles Schumer summed up the feelings of many of his party colleagues on the third day of the hearings:

> Your failure to answer questions is confounding me. It's as if I asked you 'What kind of movies do you like? Tell me two or three good movies.' And you say, 'I like movies with good acting.' Then I ask you if you like *Casablanca*,' and you respond by saying 'Lots of people like *Casablanca*.' You tell me, 'It's widely settled that *Casablanca* is one of the great movies.'

But even at this moment, Roberts got the better of his opponent. As the laughter — at Roberts's expense — died down, Chairman Arlen Specter called a recess, but Roberts asked if he could reply to Senator Schumer. '*Dr Zhivago* and *North by Northwest*,' Roberts said in a deadpan tone. As the *Washington Post* reported it: 'The crowd scored it another point for Roberts.'

In his summing up on the fourth and final day of committee hearings, Roberts declared 'I'm not an ideologue,' claiming that his loyalties are to the Constitution and the rule of law. Even some Democrats appeared to have been won over, Dianne Feinstein of California, for example, describing Roberts as 'a fine legal scholar'. After Roberts left the witness chair following 2 days of testimony, Chairman Specter announced that the routine FBI check on Roberts did not find anything that would disqualify him from serving on the Supreme Court.

The remainder of the day was given over to hearing from more than 30 witnesses who spoke for or against his confirmation. They included law professors, theologians and a female lawyer whom Roberts had helped win promotion. A representative of the American Bar Association explained why the organisation had given Roberts its highest — 'well qualified' — rating.

Roberts confirmed as 17th chief justice

Six days later the Judiciary Committee convened again to vote on the Roberts nomination. By 13 votes to 5, they recommended confirmation to the full Senate. The 13 'yes' votes included all 10 Republican committee members, plus 3 of the Democrats — Russell Feingold of Wisconsin, Herbert Kohl of Wisconsin and, most surprisingly, the ranking Democrat Patrick Leahy of Vermont.

A week later, on Thursday 29 September, the full Senate voted 78–22 to confirm John Roberts as the 17th chief justice of the United States. The vote in the Senate chamber reflected that within the committee — all 55 Republican senators voted 'yes', joined by 22 Democrats plus independent James Jeffords, while 22 Democrats voted 'no'. Hence, President Bush managed to split Senate Democrats right down the middle with the Roberts nomination (see Table 6.1 overleaf). Three hours later, at the White House swearing-in ceremony, President Bush claimed that 'the Senate has confirmed a man with an astute mind and a kind heart,' who will be 'prudent in exercising judicial power, firm in defending judicial independence and, above all, a faithful guardian of the Constitution'. Or so he hopes. And at 50, Roberts is the youngest person to hold the office since the 46-year old John Marshall back in 1801. He could, therefore, be in office for 25–30 years. Marshall, indeed, served as chief justice for 34 years. President Bush will therefore hope beyond hope that he has read Chief Justice Roberts well.

But as the *Washington Post* reminded us at the end of this whole process: 'An appointee's past has provided little or no guidance to his or her performance on the Court, thanks in part to the influence of colleagues, in part to the independence conferred by a life term, and in part to a tendency of justices to compromise, lest they dwell in the margins of the law, unable to build majorities or write opinion of consequence.'

Table 6.1 The votes of Democrat senators on the confirmation of John Roberts

Democrats voting 'yes'	Democrats voting 'no'
Max Baucus, Montana	Daniel Akaka, Hawaii
Jeff Bingaman, New Mexico	Evan Bayh, Indiana
Robert Byrd, West Virginia	Joseph Biden, Delaware
Thomas Carper, Delaware	Barbara Boxer, California
Kent Conrad, North Dakota	Maria Cantwell, Washington
Christopher Dodd, Connecticut	Hillary Clinton, New York
Byron Dorgan, North Dakota	Jon Corzine, New Jersey
Russell Feingold, Wisconsin	Mark Dayton, Minnesota
Tim Johnson, South Dakota	Dick Durbin, Illinois
Herbert Kohl, Wisconsin	Dianne Feinstein, California
Mary Landrieu, Louisiana	Tom Harkin, Iowa
Patrick Leahy, Vermont	Daniel Inouye, Hawaii
Carl Levin, Michigan	Edward Kennedy, Massachusetts
Joseph Lieberman, Connecticut	John Kerry, Massachusetts
Blanche Lincoln, Arkansas	Frank Lautenberg, New Jersey
Patty Murray, Washington	Barbara Mikulski, Maryland
Bill Nelson, Florida	Barack Obama, Illinois
Ben Nelson, Nebraska	Jack Reed, Rhode Island
Mark Pryor, Arkansas	Harry Reid, Nevada
Jay Rockefeller, West Virginia	Paul Sarbanes, Maryland
Ken Salazar, Colorado	Charles Schumer, New York
Ron Wyden, Oregon	Debbie Stabenow, Michigan

Table 6.2 Chief justices of the United States, 1789–2005

Name	Confirmed	Vote
John Jay	26 September 1789	Voice vote
John Rutledge*	15 December 1795	10–14 (rejected)
Oliver Ellsworth	4 March 1796	21–1
John Marshall	27 January 1801	Voice vote
Roger Brooke Taney	15 March 1836	29–15
Salmon Portland Chase	6 December 1864	Voice vote
Morrison Remick Waite	21 January 1874	63–0
Melville Weston Fuller	20 July 1888	41–20
Edward Douglass White	12 December 1910	Voice vote
William Howard Taft	30 June 1921	Voice vote
Charles Evans Hughes	3 February 1930	52–26
Harlan Fiske Stone	27 June 1941	Voice vote
Frederick M. Vinson	20 June 1946	Voice vote
Earl Warren	1 March 1954	Voice vote
Warren E. Burger	9 June 1969	74–3
William H. Rehnquist	17 September 1986	65–33
John G. Roberts	29 September 2005	78–22

Source: *Congressional Quarterly* p. 2651, 3 October 2005

* Served as chief justice through a recess appointment.

The Senate vote was followed by the swearing in of Roberts at a ceremony in the East Room at the White House. The Supreme Court's senior justice, John Paul Stevens, administered the oath.

Duties of the Chief Justice

- Presides over conferences at which the Supreme Court justices discuss and vote on the cases before them.
- When in the majority, decides which justice will write the Opinion of the Court.
- Traditionally, administers the oath of office taken by the president at the inauguration ceremony.
- Presides over the trial of a US president before the Senate following an impeachment.

The Rehnquist legacy

William Hubbs Rehnquist served on the Supreme Court for 33 years 8 months and 23 days. Only six Supreme Court justices had served for longer in the Court's 216-year history. Born in 1924, Rehnquist earned degrees in political science and law from Stanford and Harvard before becoming a clerk to Supreme Court Justice Robert Jackson in 1952. The following year he moved to Arizona, where in 1964 he became involved in the ill-fated presidential campaign of Arizona Senator Barry Goldwater. When Nixon entered the White House in 1969, Rehnquist was appointed Assistant Attorney General. Two years later, Nixon nominated him to the Supreme Court to fill the vacancy caused by the retirement of Associate Justice John Harlan. Rehnquist was himself a little surprised to be nominated. As Nixon was trying to decide who to nominate, Rehnquist joked to a journalist that he had 'no chance at all' of being nominated because 'I'm not from the South, I'm not a woman, and I'm not mediocre'. The Senate confirmed him in a vote of 68–26.

Rehnquist dissented in the case of *Roe* v. *Wade*, which gave women in the USA a constitutional right to have an abortion. Elevated to Chief Justice in 1986 by President Reagan, the Senate again confirmed him, this time by 65 votes to 33. In 1999 he presided over the impeachment trial of President Clinton, only the second chief justice to be called upon to fulfil this role. He continued on the Court right up until his death, thus becoming the first Supreme Court justice to die in office for over 50 years — the last was Fred Vinson, who died in September 1953.

Although the Supreme Court which Rehnquist joined back in 1972 was appointed mostly by Republican presidents — there were only three Democrat appointees — the Court's majority was of a liberal philosophy. Indeed, the young Rehnquist once described two of his fellow Republican appointees Earl Warren and Hugo Black as 'left-wing philosophers'. As a new member of the Supreme Court, Rehnquist became known as the 'Lone Ranger' because he was so often the sole dissenter among the nine members. Not only was he one of only two justices to dissent in *Roe* v. *Wade*, but he was the only justice to say in 1983 that Bob Jones University could not be denied tax-exempt status because of alleged racial discrimination.

Key word

strict constructionist: describes the view that judges should interpret the Constitution in a strict, literal or conservative fashion; that judges should not 'make law', but should leave that to the legislature.

In these and similar decisions, Rehnquist was motivated by his **strict constructionist** views and his opposition to the idea that the Supreme Court existed to establish the 'fairness' that some thought lacking in contemporary American society. If 'fairness' needed addressing, that, in Rehnquist's view, was a job for legislators not judges — for Congress, not the Supreme Court. In an interview with Fox News in 2001, Rehnquist put it this way:

> For the courts to come along and say, 'We just don't like what happened here. We think it's "unjust"', is giving them a rather subjective mandate that I think many people, if they fully understood it, would find troubling.

Rehnquist believed that the Supreme Court under chief justices Earl Warren and Warren Burger had gone beyond what the framers of the post-Civil War 14th Amendment had intended in guaranteeing 'equal protection of the laws' by state governments. Rehnquist felt that this amendment was meant merely to forbid a narrow range of discriminatory conduct.

But as Rehnquist's years on the Court passed, not only did appointments by Presidents Ronald Reagan (1981–89) and George Bush (1989-93) swing the views of the Court's majority more in line with Rehnquist's, but the prevailing views within US society also moved in Rehnquist's direction. The liberalism of the 1960s and 1970s gave way to more conservative views in the last two decades of the twentieth century. With the confirmation of Clarence Thomas in 1991, Rehnquist had the five usually conservative votes he needed to put his views of the law into effect, supported by Scalia, O'Connor, Kennedy and Thomas. The Lone Ranger had become part of the Federalist Five, as Rehnquist and his fellow conservatives were known. It was the Federalist Five, led by Chief Justice Rehnquist, who issued a series of rulings during the 1990s that struck down efforts by Congress to subject state governments to laws protecting women against domestic violence, banning guns near school property and prohibiting discrimination against disabled workers.

To his critics, Rehnquist was a reactionary, trying to roll back the power of the federal government. To supporters, he was restoring the proper and intended balance of power between the federal and state governments. But whichever side of the argument you were on, there was no mistaking that Rehnquist was the driving force. John C. Jeffries, Dean of the University of Virginia Law School, stated that 'you can't identify anyone who's had more to do with the revival of federalism than Bill Rehnquist'.

A recent decision that probably most pleased Rehnquist was his majority opinion in *Zelman* v. *Simmons-Harris* (2002). In upholding Ohio's school voucher programme, the Supreme Court made a clear statement in favour of states' rights over the power of the federal government as well as taking a less rigid view of the separation between church and state. Both of these positions were clearly those of Chief Justice Rehnquist. Writing in the majority opinion, Rehnquist stated:

> The question is whether Ohio is coercing parents into sending their children to religious schools, and that question must be answered evaluating all options Ohio provides Cleveland school children, only one of which is to obtain a [voucher] and then choose a religious school.

But Rehnquist's legacy was a limited one. In the view of Charles Lane (*Washington Post*, 4 September 2005), Rehnquist's impact was 'blunted by his inability to win over the Court's vital centre, as represented by fellow Republican appointees Sandra Day O'Connor and Anthony Kennedy'. Thus on many major decisions Rehnquist found himself in the minority. Table 6.3 considers 10 major Supreme Court decisions during Rehnquist's tenure as chief justice.

Case	Concerning	Decision	Rehnquist's position
Texas v. *Johnson* (1989)	Texas state law forbidding flag burning declared unconstitutional	5–4	Minority
US v. *Lopez* (1995)	Gun-Free School Zones Act declared unconstitutional	5–4	**Majority**
Reno v. *ACLU* (1997)	Communications Decency Act declared unconstitutional	7–2	Minority
Bush v. *Gore* (2000)	Stopped Florida recount in 2000 presidential election	5–4	**Majority**
Ashcroft v. *Free Speech Coalition* (2002)	Child Pornography Protection Act declared unconstitutional	7–2	Minority
Zelman v. *Simmons-Harris* (2002)	Upheld Ohio school voucher programme	5–4	**Majority**
Atkins v. *Virginia* (2002)	Execution of mentally retarded declared constitutional	6–3	Minority
Gratz v. *Bollinger* (2003)	University of Michigan undergraduate admissions affirmative action programme declared unconstitutional	6–3	**Majority**
Grutter v. *Bollinger* (2003)	Upheld University of Michigan Law School admissions affirmative action programme	5–4	Minority
McConnell v. *FECA* (2004)	Upheld Bipartisan Campaign Reform Act	5–4	Minority

Table 6.3 Rehnquist's position in selected landmark decisions

In only four of these cases was Rehnquist in the majority. Thus Rehnquist lost in a number of cases about which he cared deeply, including freedom of speech (*Reno* v. *ACLU*, *Ashcroft* v. *Free Speech Coalition* and *McConnell* v. *FEC*), the death penalty (*Atkins* v. *Virginia*) and affirmative action (*Grutter* v. *Bollinger*).

When in the latter case the Supreme Court upheld the University of Michigan Law School's affirmative action programme, Rehnquist described the decision as a 'naked effort to achieve racial balancing', seeing it as 'a carefully managed programme designed to ensure proportionate representation of applicants from selected minority groups'.

Rehnquist was equally scathing of the Court's 2004 decision to uphold the Bipartisan Campaign Reform Act in *McConnell* v. *FECA*. In his minority opinion, Rehnquist argued:

> No doubt Congress was convinced by the many abuses of the current [campaign finance] system that something in this area must be done. Its response, however, was too blunt.

Georgetown Law Professor Mark Tushnet, whose recently published book, *A Court Divided: The Rehnquist Court and the Future of Constitutional Law* (Norton, 2005), is a readable and scholarly analysis of the Court over which Rehnquist presided for nearly 20 years, has the last word.

> When the history of the Supreme Court in the twentieth century is written, there will be two great chief justices: Earl Warren and William Rehnquist. Both presided over courts that changed the law in a very dramatic way.

Exercises

1 How long a period had elapsed without any vacancies to the Supreme Court by the time Sandra Day O'Connor announced her retirement?
2 Who was nominated by President Bush to fill this vacancy on the Supreme Court?
3 Give a brief summary of John Roberts's career.
4 How did Democrats react to the nomination of John Roberts to the Supreme Court?
5 What event occurred on 3 September 2005?
6 Why did President Bush decide to nominate John Roberts to fill this new vacancy?
7 What was John Roberts trying to achieve by his remarks to the Senate Judiciary Committee in which he described judges as 'umpires'?
8 What was the press reaction to Roberts's performance at the Senate Judiciary Committee?
9 What did Roberts mean by the statement 'I'm not an ideologue'?
10 What were the votes on the Roberts nomination (a) in the Senate Judiciary Committee and (b) in the Senate chamber? How did the two parties vote?
11 What is significant about the fact that Roberts was only 50 years old when confirmed as chief justice?

12 Give a brief summary of William Rehnquist's career.
13 Why was Rehnquist known as the 'Lone Ranger' in the 1970s?
14 What two reasons are suggested for Rehnquist's views gradually becoming the majority views of the Supreme Court?
15 What does Table 6.3 tell us about the limits of Rehnquist's legacy?

Chapter 7

Ronald Reagan 25 years on

On 20 January 1981 — just 25 years ago — I stood on Pennsylvania Avenue in Washington DC, outside the headquarters of the FBI, to watch the inauguration of Ronald Reagan as the fortieth president of the USA. Reagan was coming to the presidency just days away from his seventieth birthday — the oldest president in the USA's 200-year history. His opponents had quipped that Reagan was 'a president for the '80s — the over 80s!' Reagan would have enjoyed the joke. He died on 5 June 2004, aged 93.

I had arrived in Washington a couple of days before the ceremony. The weather had been so cold for so long that the Potomac river — as wide as the Thames in London — was frozen solid from bank to bank. The temperature had been below freezing for nearly a month. The day I arrived, the daytime high was –15°C. But suddenly, on 20 January, warmer winds arrived from the south to shut out the Arctic blasts and the temperature shot up more than 30 degrees. It seemed positively spring-like.

That seemed something of an omen, for the nation had passed through a dark winter during the previous decade: the Vietnam War; the Watergate scandal and subsequent resignation of President Nixon; the energy crisis; the 'failed' one-term presidencies of Gerald Ford and Jimmy Carter. And to cap it all, this day marked the 444th day of a hostage crisis that had begun in November 1979, during which time 52 Americans had been held in Tehran by revolutionary 'students' protesting against US policy towards Iran. And onto this stage walked this big man, with a big heart and a big vision.

What was Reagan's legacy as president? How is he remembered? What were his achievements? How could someone who had once starred in a Hollywood film alongside a chimpanzee (*Bedtime for Bonzo* was the film's illustrious title) become president of the USA?

The path to the presidency

Ronald Wilson Reagan was born on 6 February 1911 in Tampico, Illinois, in the front bedroom of a five-room flat above the general store in Main Street where his father worked. Even these circumstances became synonymous with the man. Reagan as a politician never lost his ability to resonate with Main Street America. When he moved into the White House he quipped that he was used to 'living above the shop'.

His childhood was, like the USA, a mixture of the idyllic and the tragic. In his autobiography, *Where's the Rest of Me?* (the title is a line from another Reagan film, *Kings Row*), Reagan wrote of his boyhood as being 'a rare Huckleberry Finn idyll' of exploring woods and meadows, and enjoying escapades and pick-up games of soccer with other boys. The darker side of the young Ronald's life came from his alcoholic father. His autobiography describes a scene of him as an 11-year-old finding his father 'drunk, dead to the world', lying in the snow by the porch of the family house in Dixon, Illinois, and of the young son dragging his father into the house and up to bed. For the rest of his life, Reagan shared his mother's distaste for alcohol.

The Reagans were certainly not wealthy and were almost overwhelmed by the effects of the Great Depression, which hit when Ronald was in his late teens and early twenties. Again, this experience showed up in his later political career with a genuine understanding for the hardships of unemployment. Reagan would frequently tell the story of when his salesman father opened a letter on Christmas Eve expecting a bonus and found out instead that he had been fired. Of his family's plight during the 1930s, Reagan would later comment: 'We didn't live on the wrong side of the tracks, but we lived so close to them we could hear the whistle real loud.' Through it all, Reagan displayed the sparkling optimism that characterised his whole life. 'Life is just one grand sweet song, so start the music,' he once wrote.

After graduating from a small college near Peoria, Illinois, in 1932, Reagan got a job in radio as a sports announcer in Des Moines, Iowa, before finding his way into Hollywood films in 1937. During the next 20 years he made 52 films, playing in most of them 'the heart-warming role of himself', as social historian Garry Wills so accurately put it. In 1940 he married his first wife, the actress Jane Wyman, but the marriage ended in divorce in less than a decade. In 1952 he married another actress, Nancy Davis, their marriage spanning the remaining 52 years of his life.

Reagan emerged onto the national political stage with a polished and patriotic speech on behalf of Barry Goldwater, the Republican presidential candidate in 1964. Elected Governor of California in 1966, he served two terms, leaving office in 1974. In 1976, he challenged Gerald Ford for the Republican presidential nomination. Ford had become vice-president by appointment in 1973 and then president in 1974 following Nixon's resignation. Reagan mounted a strong challenge to the incumbent president and came within 120 votes — out of over 2,000 — of defeating Ford for the nomination at the 1976 Republican National Convention. Four years later, he was the clear front-runner for his party's presidential nomination, which he won comfortably, going on to defeat incumbent President Jimmy Carter by 489–49 votes in the Electoral College.

His presidential campaign was almost flawless. Admittedly, Jimmy Carter was weighed down with huge problems — rampant inflation, high unemployment, spiralling energy costs and a year-long hostage crisis. To some extent, all Reagan had to do was show up and say: 'Hi, I'm the guy who isn't Jimmy Carter.' But his margin of victory over an incumbent president evidenced a politician of unusual standing. Throughout the campaign, Reagan exuded boundless optimism.

The most memorable moment was the one televised debate between Carter and Reagan in the campaign's final week. While the President looked harassed, Reagan appeared jaunty and relaxed. Each attack on him by Carter brought the same response: cocking his head to one side, smiling broadly and with a chuckle, Reagan would say to the President, 'There you go again!' Then there was the masterful series of questions that Reagan posed to the television audience, which included the line: 'Are you better off than you were 4 years ago?' You could criticise this for being a selfish way of looking at the electoral issues, but the Reagan team knew that it would resonate to their advantage with millions of ordinary voters — Republicans, Democrats and independents. The look on Carter's face as Reagan spoke these lines gave him the appearance of a naughty pet dog who had just been hit over the head with a rolled-up newspaper. He went on to lose 44 states — and the election — to Ronald Reagan.

The presidency that nearly wasn't

It was the seventieth day of the administration of the 70-year-old president. On the afternoon of 30 March 1981, the President had just finished addressing a labour union conference at the Washington Hilton Hotel, less than a mile from the White House. Reagan emerged from a rear door off the hotel ballroom into the bright sunlight of a Washington spring day to walk a matter of a few yards to his waiting car. Suddenly shots rang out. In seconds, the President's press officer had been shot in the head and the President, unknown to himself, had a bullet lodged inches from his left lung.

The Secret Service bundled the President head-first into the back of the waiting limousine and landed on top of him. Reagan felt a pain and thought he might have cracked a rib when he landed face down in the car. Then he realised he was coughing blood. The car, now racing down 16th Street back to the safety of the White House, was detoured to the George Washington University Hospital, six blocks to the west. By the time his wife arrived from the White House, the President had an oxygen mask over his face and was being rushed to the operating theatre to have the near-fatal bullet removed. 'Sorry, Honey, I forgot to duck!' he cracked at Nancy Reagan. As the medical team gathered round him he enquired: 'I hope all you doctors are Republicans!' In the words of *Boston Globe* columnist David Nyhan: 'Reagan won our hearts that day. He almost became JFK but settled for John Wayne, becoming a legend with a wince and a wisecrack.' Within weeks he was back at his Oval Office desk. The reception he received when he addressed a joint session of Congress later that summer was a cross between a pop concert and the arrival of the Pope!

Cashing in his political capital

Having defeated an incumbent president by a substantial margin and survived an attempt on his life, Reagan set about cashing in his political capital. His wasn't so much a honeymoon as a love-fest. His Republicans controlled the Senate — for the first time in 26 years — and in the House he could often put together a winning coalition by persuading 20 or so southern conservative Democrats to support the Republican minority. Reagan's communication skills were legendary. He was the person who 'could sell ice to Eskimos'. He was 'the Great Communicator', although David Broder of the *Washington Post* always thought this title wasn't quite right, and later wrote:

> The reason that Reagan was persuasive, I came to understand, was that he had first persuaded himself of the truth of his utterances. When someone hung the title of 'The Great Communicator' on Reagan, I thought to myself, 'It should be "The Great Persuader".'

And he somehow persuaded a Democratic-controlled House of Representatives and a deeply sceptical House Speaker, Tip O'Neill, to agree to huge tax cuts along with massive increases in defence spending.

The secret of his success

Reagan was often underestimated. There were certainly those who regarded him as lightweight, lacking in any grasp of policy detail. People poked fun at his work habits — his late starts and early finishes, and the fact that he liked to take naps during the day. He was fond of commenting that he knew hard work never killed anyone, before adding with a smile, 'but I figure, why take the chance?' There was a persistent rumour that he had fallen asleep in a cabinet meeting. His forgetfulness caused more raised eyebrows. He once mistook one of his cabinet officers for a visiting city mayor. The 'cue cards' from which he gave his speeches were legendary.

Humour was an important part of the way Reagan got alongside people and broke the ice. Cabinet meetings, I was told, always began with Reagan telling some joke or anecdote. Some of his humour was spontaneous, and it was often self-deprecating. Asked while visiting US astronauts in Houston, before the successful launch of the space shuttle *Discovery* in 1988, whether he would like to go into space, Reagan joked: 'I've been in space for several years.' In one State of the Union Address to Congress, he began by quoting Thomas Jefferson, one of the nation's Founding Fathers, and then added: 'I would just like to point out to members of the press who I know put such a premium on accuracy that I did not actually hear Thomas Jefferson say those words.' And there was his quip at the start of the second televised debate with Walter Mondale in 1984. Reagan had been asked whether he was too old to be president. Reagan, dead-pan, replied: 'I want you to know that I will not use age as an issue in this campaign. I will not exploit for political purposes my

opponent's youth and inexperience.' Even Mondale succumbed to genuine laughter. It remains the best joke told in a presidential debate.

Reagan also exuded confidence. By the end of the 1970s, commentators were discussing whether the presidency was still a manageable office. The Imperial Presidency of Johnson and Nixon had, according to many commentators, turned into the 'imperilled presidency' under Ford and Carter, and some doubted whether anyone could now do the job. But Reagan arrived, looked around and said: 'This is fun, let's saddle up and go for a ride.' Reagan wanted to transfer his confidence to others. 'What I'd really like to do is go down in history as the president who made Americans believe in themselves again,' he remarked early in his first term. Reagan was the eternal optimist. He never dwelt on negatives. The glass was always half-full rather than half-empty. Even when he wrote a letter to the nation in 1994 informing the people that he had succumbed to Alzheimer's disease, it ended: 'I know that for America there will always be a bright dawn ahead.'

He had a clear vision of what he wanted to achieve and announced his ambitions in such a devastatingly simple fashion that many thought them simplistic and idealistic. But Reagan believed that if you wanted to move mountains, then a good way of achieving this was by announcing that mountain moving was the name of the game. Speaking to a joint session of the UK parliament in June 1982, Reagan announced that the Soviet Union would wind up on 'the ash heap of history'. In June 1987, standing in front of the Brandenburg Gate near the Berlin Wall, Reagan announced: 'Mr Gorbachev, open this gate! Mr Gorbachev, tear down this wall!' It sounded ridiculous, and many opponents and commentators wasted no time in saying so. But 10 months after Reagan left office, the Berlin Wall was dismantled. And in 1991, Gorbachev stepped down and the Soviet Union — and the Cold War — became history. No, I am not suggesting that Reagan single-handedly won the Cold War or caused the Soviet Union to implode. But it is credible to suggest that he hastened the occurrence of both events.

Asked by a reporter on the eve of the 1980 election what Americans saw in him, Reagan replied: 'Would you laugh if I told you that I think, maybe, they see themselves, and that I'm one of them?' Reagan always described himself as a 'citizen politician'. And having convinced people that he was not really a politician at all, he then convinced them that they could trust him — unlike politicians. Gary Hart, a Democrat senator, once remarked that Reagan was successful 'not because he is the Great Communicator but because he has values and ideas and acts upon them'. And this was in tune with Reagan's self-image. Here is part of his farewell address to the US people at the very end of his presidency:

> I never thought it was my style or the words I used that made a difference. It was the content. I wasn't a great communicator, but I communicated great

things, and they didn't spring full bloom from my brow, they came from the heart of a great nation — from our experience, our wisdom and our belief in the principles that have guided us for two centuries.

Foreign policy: success and failure

Writing just after Reagan's death, conservative commentator George Will had this to say:

> One measure of a leader's greatness is this: By the time he dies, the dangers that summoned him to greatness have been so thoroughly defeated, in no small measure by what he did, it is difficult to recall the magnitude of those dangers or of his achievements. So if you seek Ronald Reagan's monument, look around and consider what you do not see. The Iron Curtain that scarred a continent is gone, as is the Evil Empire responsible for it.

During Reagan's first term, he held no meetings with the Soviet leadership. When asked the reason, Reagan commented that 'they keep dying on me!' Brezhnev, Andropov and Chernenko were passing players. But then came the reform-minded Mikhail Gorbachev. Beginning in 1985, Reagan and Gorbachev held five summits, the most productive being the one in Washington in 1987 when they signed the Intermediate-Range Nuclear Forces (INF) Treaty, the first agreement between the USA and the USSR to cut their respective nuclear arsenals. All previous agreements had merely been about limiting the increases.

When a West German nightclub frequented by US servicemen was blown up by a terrorist's bomb in 1986, Reagan — with the support of the British Prime Minister, Margaret Thatcher — bombed Libya, the supposed perpetrators. Libya's Colonel Gaddafi began to cut his links with international terrorist organisations, a transformation that was completed just last year.

Another success was the Soviet withdrawal from Afghanistan, although this opened the door for the Taliban regime to exert its deadly influence. This was ended by the current Bush administration. Afghanistan now has an elected government.

But there were failures. In October 1983, 241 marines were killed when their barracks were bombed in Lebanon. The deployment had been widely criticised, and following the deaths of so many US service personnel in one attack, the remainder were 'redeployed'.

The most significant foreign policy debacle came in November 1986 with disclosures that Reagan had secretly approved an arms deal with Iran in an attempt to win the release of US hostages held in Lebanon. Things were made worse when it was revealed that the proceeds of the arms deal had been sent to help the Contra rebels in Nicaragua in their fight against the Marxist Sandinista government. So was born the so-called Iran–Contra affair, which led to the sacking of Reagan's National Security Advisor, John Poindexter, and the National Security Council staff aide Oliver North, who was accused of masterminding the whole affair. It also led to the downfall of White House Chief of Staff Donald Regan.

The Iran–Contra affair was a failure of both policy and process. Congress had passed a law forbidding any arms deals with the Iranians and another which forbade any support for the Contra rebels in Nicaragua. Congress established a select committee to investigate the matter and the President appointed an independent commission, under the chairmanship of former Texas senator John Tower, to do the same.

The Tower Commission report was published in February 1987 and was scathing of the administration's policy and the policy-making process:

> The National Security Council (NSC) staff seemed to be running the operation. The President appeared to be unaware of key elements of the operation. It is important to emphasise that the President is responsible for the national security policy of the United States. In the development and execution of that policy, the President is the decision-maker. The NSC system will not work unless the President makes it work. By his actions, by his leadership, the President determines the quality of its performance.

But the most stinging criticism was reserved for the White House Chief of Staff, Don Regan:

> Mr Regan also shares in this responsibility. More than almost any Chief of Staff of recent memory, he asserted personal control over the White House staff and sought to extend this control to the National Security Advisor. He was personally active in national security affairs and attended almost all of the relevant meetings regarding the Iran initiative. He must bear primary responsibility for the chaos that descended upon the White House.

Having received and studied the report, President Reagan went on prime-time television to address the nation. Even in his worst crisis, Reagan's well-tuned antennae for public opinion and expectations did not fail him. What the public wanted to hear was an admission of an error of judgement and the President taking personal responsibility. After some brief opening remarks, Reagan cut to the chase:

> First, let me say I take full responsibility for my actions and for those of my administration. As angry as I may be about activities undertaken without my knowledge, I am still accountable for those activities. As disappointed as I may be in some who served me, I am still the one who must answer to the American people for this behaviour. As the Navy would say, this happened on my watch. There are reasons why it happened, but no excuses. It was a mistake.

Had either Richard Nixon over Watergate or Bill Clinton over Monica Lewinsky ever addressed the American people with such candour from the outset, their personal histories might have turned out somewhat differently. Reagan was a rarity — a politician who knew that using the words 'full responsibility' and 'mistake' is the only way to repair political damage in a self-inflicted crisis. More than they hate mistakes, what citizens really hate is a cover-up and lack of candour. Reagan was a big enough person to say what he needed to say. Nixon before him had lied to cover up the mistakes. Clinton after him debated the meaning of the word 'is', thereby trying to wriggle out of personal responsibility. When a recent piece of research was conducted about the moral authority of former presidents while in office, Ronald Reagan came in eleventh (out of 41). Nixon and Clinton came in respectively fortieth and forty-first!

Reagan's legacy

To his critics, Reagan's biggest legacy was the soaring federal budget deficit, which would take two decades to reduce. These critics saw Reagan as a hands-off president whose intellectual limitations led him to have a scant grasp of policy and thereby become too reliant upon senior staff and advisers. They saw him as simplistic and rather dangerous. To them, his unbreakable belief in 'Star Wars' technology symbolised this.

To his admirers, Reagan was to the Republican Party in the 1980s what Franklin D. Roosevelt had been to the Democrats in the 1930s. He reshaped Republican Party politics and led to the break-up of the Democrats' solid south. 'Beginning with FDR, the presumption was that if you had a problem, the federal government was going to solve it,' remarked David Keene of the American Conservative Union. 'Beginning with Reagan, the presumption was that if you had a problem, government was likely to screw things up and you looked for a private solution.'

Reagan broke up the old Democrat 'New Deal Coalition' — of which he, ironically, had once been a part. The 1980s saw a new term enter the US political dictionary — 'Reagan Democrats'. According to the *Washington Post*'s Dan Balz, Reagan's 'social conservatism, his unapologetic appeals to patriotism, his challenge to the Soviets and his economic policies brought one-time Democrats streaming into the Republican column.' Unlike either Bill Clinton (1996) or George W. Bush (2004), Reagan won re-election in 1984 by a landslide with 60% of the popular vote, winning 49 states. Reagan's appeal was to blue-collar workers, some labour unions, the south and young people — all traditionally Democrat-voting groups. According to Ralph Reed: '…it is undeniable that the Republican Party of today is largely the party that he remade — a conservative, grass-roots party, and one whose candidates, with very few exceptions, pledge fealty to the principles that he articulated.'

Reagan's political and electoral success forced the US Democratic Party to do what Margaret Thatcher's success has forced the British Labour Party to do. In 1992, with Bill Clinton and Al Gore, the Democrats shed their big government, tax-and-spend, liberal image. But the evidence of the 2000 and 2004 US elections would suggest that the Democrats have not carried out nearly as successful a reformation as New Labour did under Tony Blair in the UK.

'Actor, Governor, President, Icon,' was how Lou Cannon remembered Reagan. And the eminent political historian James MacGregor Burns, best known for his books about FDR, stated in the *Washington Post* that Reagan would rank with FDR among the 'great' or 'near-great' presidents of the twentieth century. To his old rival Mikhail Gorbachev, Reagan was 'a really big person — a very great political leader'. It's an assessment that will infuriate Reagan's critics, but please his admirers.

Exercises

1. Give a brief description of Ronald Reagan's early life, before he entered politics in the 1960s
2. What event brought Reagan to national notice in 1964?
3. To what post was Reagan elected in 1966?
4. How near did Reagan come to winning the Republican Party's presidential nomination in 1976?
5. Describe some of the events that led to Reagan winning the 1980 presidential election.
6. What event occurred on 30 March 1981, and how did it affect Reagan's presidency?
7. What phrase does David Broder use to describe Ronald Reagan?
8. What factors does the chapter suggest were the ingredients of Reagan's success?
9. How does George Will suggest that one can best assess a president's greatness?
10. What were the notable foreign policy successes of Reagan's presidency?
11. What was the Iran–Contra affair, and what weaknesses did it show up in the Reagan administration?
12. How did Reagan avoid the Iran–Contra affair becoming a more serious problem for his presidency?
13. Suggest two lasting legacies of Reagan's years in office?

News from Washington DC

Pardons are now a rarity...

President George W. Bush is lagging behind his predecessors in the issuing of presidential pardons. He has thus far issued only 39 pardons and sentence commutations in just under 5 years. To put that in context, his father handed out 77 pardons during his 4-year term (1989–93). Bill Clinton chalked up no fewer than 456 in 8 years, including 176 on his last day in office! The Pardoner-in-Chief of all time remains President Franklin Roosevelt (1933–45), who in just over 12 years managed 3,678 pardons. Among those to benefit most recently from George W. Bush's pardons was Joseph Warner of McLaughlin, South Dakota, who had been sentenced to 8 months imprisonment, a $5,000 fine and restitution of $5,560 back in 1995 for committing arson on an Indian reservation.

...and so are vetoes

On 20 January 2005, George W. Bush became the first president to serve a full 4-year term without vetoing a single piece of legislation since Martin van Buren, who occupied the White House between 1837 and 1841!

Iowa and New Hampshire's 'first-in-the-nation' status threatened

Following the unsuccessful presidential campaign of Senator John Kerry in 2004, the Democrats have taken yet another look at the process by which they select their presidential candidate. There have been numerous such investigations ever since the famous McGovern–Fraser Commission, which followed the party's 1968 defeat. The new commission, with the less-than-catchy title of the Commission on Presidential Nomination Timing and Scheduling, was co-chaired by Congressman David Price of North Carolina and former Clinton Labor Secretary Alexis Herman. The two issues that the Commission sought to address were front loading and the 'first-in-the-nation' status of the Iowa caucuses and New Hampshire primary. There is a school of thought that believes that Iowa and New Hampshire — two tiny, unrepresentative states — have far too prominent a role in the presidential nomination process.

Under the plan announced in mid December 2005, Iowa's caucuses would be held on 14 January 2008, one week earlier than in 2004. There would then be one or two more caucuses conducted a few days later. Then, following the New

Hampshire primary on 22 January, there would be one or two more primaries within the next week. The Commission further recommended that no more than five states be allowed to hold contests within any single week. That would eliminate 'Super Tuesday', traditionally the first Tuesday in March, when 10 states voted in 2004. The Democrats also want additional delegates awarded to states that opt to hold their primaries or caucuses later in the cycle, with those waiting until May or early June receiving the most bonus delegates.

Although the plan did not go as far as some would have liked in taking away the privileged positions of Iowa and New Hampshire as the 'first in the nation' caucus and primary, Senator Carl Levin of Michigan said that he hoped 'it's the beginning of the end' for Iowa and New Hampshire: 'It's a crack in the wall which New Hampshire and Iowa have built around their privilege. I think the wall sooner or later will come tumbling down, and should.' However, all one can say is that previous attempts to reform the presidential candidate nominating process have proved somewhat ineffective at halting the slide towards front loading and quick decisions.

Third Party votes in 2004

The Federal Election Commission has now reported the final tally of votes for all parties that contested the 2004 presidential election. George W. Bush polled 62,028,285 votes (or 50.75% of the vote) while John Kerry polled 59,028,109 votes (or 48.27% of the vote). The votes cast for third party candidates were as follows:

Ralph Nader	Independent	463,647	0.38%
Michael Badnarik	Libertarian Party	397,234	0.32%
Michael Peroutka	Constitution Party	143,609	0.12%
David Cobb	Green Party	119,862	0.10%
Write-in votes	[Miscellaneous]	37,190	0.03%
Leonard Peltier	Peace and Freedom Party	27,607	0.02%
Walter Brown	Socialist Party USA	10,822	0.01%
James Harris	Socialist Workers Party	7,433	0.01%
Roger Calero	Socialist Workers Party	3,689	0.00%
None of these candidates	[Nevada ballot option]	3,688	0.00%
Thomas Harens	Christian Freedom Party	2,387	0.00%
Gene Amondson	Concerns of People Party	1,944	0.00%
Bill Van Auken	Socialist Equality Party	1,857	0.00%
John Parker	Workers World Party	1,646	0.00%
Charles Jay	Personal Choice Party	946	0.00%
Stanford Andress	Unaffiliated	804	0.00%
Earl Dodge	Prohibition Party	140	0.00%

Note: the total number of votes cast in the election was 122,280,899.

New party chairs...

Both the two major parties have selected new national chairs following the 2004 elections. The new chair of the Republican National Committee is **Ken Mehlman**, while his opposite number at the Democratic National Committee is **Howard Dean**.

...and more new executive branch appointments

Meanwhile President Bush has appointed Indiana businessman **Allan Hubbard** as the head of the National Economic Council (NEC). Hubbard is a Bush crony — both an old friend and fundraiser. The NEC was created in 1993 by Bill Clinton. Hubbard becomes the sixth person to head the Council in its first 12 years. In another economic policy appointment, the President nominated **Ben Bernanke** to succeed Alan Greenspan as chairman of the Federal Reserve Board. Bernanke had previously served as chairman of the Council of Economic Advisers within the Executive Office of the President. In the area of defence policy, **General Peter Pace** was nominated by the President to succeed General Richard Myers as chairman of the Joint Chiefs of Staff, the highest post in the armed forces.

The new Bush administration by numbers

Take the top 367 officials in the second Bush administration — in the White House, cabinet departments and independent agencies — and what do you find? The answer is that they are overwhelmingly white (83%), male (73%) and married (86%). The average age is 51 — the youngest is 25, the oldest 83. But there are some surprises. As to the region of the country where they grew up, the most common is the northeast (27%), followed by the Midwest (23%) and then the south (22%). And 13% of these top 367 previously worked in the Clinton administration.

State of the Union Address

President Bush delivered his 2005 State of the Union speech to a joint session of Congress on 2 February. The centrepiece of the speech was the President's request that Congress move forward on reform of the social security retirement system to avoid it becoming bankrupt as the USA's population gets older. The President stated: 'Social security was a great moral success of the twentieth century and we must honour its great purposes in this new century.' The President immediately embarked on a five-state tour to promote his social security reform plan, focusing on the states of Democratic senators where he had won the presidential vote in 2004, three of whom are up for re-election in the 2006 mid-term elections.

A mixed bag for the President in Congress

While social security reform legislation remained bogged down in Congress for much of the year, the President did gain a few successes for his legislative programme. On 18 February, Bush signed the **Class Action Fairness Act** into law, which is intended to limit class-action lawsuits by transferring them from state to federal courts. In April, the President signed the **Bankruptcy Reform Act** into law after a bipartisan vote in both houses of Congress. The Senate passed the legislation by 74 votes to 25, while the House vote was 302 to 126. The President also signed major **energy and transportation bills** into law during August.

Presidential league tables

C-SPAN, the cable television channel that provides coverage of Congress, has recently published its league tables of presidents — not including the current incumbent. There are seven categories as well as an overall tally. Four modern presidents made it into the top half of the table in the overall category: Kennedy (8th), Johnson (10th), Reagan (11th) and Bush (20th). Bill Clinton (21st) just missed the cut, and closely made it in ahead of Carter (22nd), Ford (23rd) and Nixon (25th). Taking just those eight presidents who held office between 1961 and 2001, here are the best and the worst in the seven categories:

Category	Highest placed (out of 41)	Lowest placed (out of 41)
International relations	Richard Nixon (8th)	Lyndon Johnson (36th)
Relations with Congress	Ronald Reagan (8th)	Bill Clinton (36th)
Vision/agenda setting	Ronald Reagan (8th)	Gerald Ford (31st)
Administrative skills	Lyndon Johnson (9th)	Ronald Reagan (32nd)
Public persuasion	Ronald Reagan (4th)	Gerald Ford (31st)
Crisis leadership	John Kennedy (8th)	Jimmy Carter (28th)
Moral authority	Jimmy Carter (10th)	Bill Clinton (41st)

Although not to be taken too seriously, the research does show that presidential power has many different facets to it. Even Richard Nixon and Jimmy Carter had their strengths, and Bill Clinton (41st out of 41 in the moral authority category) had his weaknesses!

Constitutional amendments fail in Congress

During the past 3 years there have been four votes in Congress — all in the House of Representatives — attempting to propose constitutional amendments. Two attempts to propose an amendment to ban desecration of the US flag both gained the necessary two-thirds majority. On 3 June 2003 the vote was 300–125, and on 22 June 2005 it was 286–130. On 2 June 2004, a proposal to introduce an amendment to permit Congress to continue in session in the event of large numbers of its members being killed was defeated 63–353. On 30 September 2004, a proposal to add a same-sex marriage ban to the Constitution failed by 227–186, 49 votes short of the two-thirds majority required.

Congressional salaries

Members of Congress received a 1.9% salary increase in 2005, taking their annual salary to $165,200 (around £90,000).

Senate filibusters

The ongoing saga of Democrats in the Senate filibustering some of President Bush's judicial nominees took a new twist in May 2005. After the Senate Majority Leader, Bill Frist, had threatened 'the nuclear option' — changing the Senate rules to abolish filibusters against judicial nominees — a bipartisan group of 14 senators reached a compromise that averted a crisis in the Senate on this issue. The 14 (7 Democrats and 7 Republicans) agreed that a filibuster would be used against a judicial nomination only in 'extraordinary circumstances'. The 14 senators who signed the agreement are mostly known for their moderate, centrist views. Five of the 7 Democrats come from red states, i.e. states won by the Republicans in the 2004 presidential election.

Senators who joined the filibuster compromise

Republicans	Democrats
Lincoln Chafee (Rhode Island)	Robert Byrd (West Virginia)
Susan Collins (Maine)	Daniel Inouye (Hawaii)
Mike De Wine (Ohio)	Mary Landrieu (Louisiana)
Lindsey Graham (South Carolina)	Joseph Lieberman (Connecticut)
John McCain (Arizona)	Ben Nelson (Nebraska)
Olympia Snow (Maine)	Mark Pryor (Arkansas)
John Warner (Virginia)	Ken Salazar (Colorado)

But the next month there was a filibuster on the President's nomination of John Bolton as ambassador to the United Nations. The cloture (or closure) vote to end debate was 54–38, six votes short of the 60 votes (three fifths of the entire Senate) required. One Republican, George Voinovich (Ohio), sided with the Democrats, while three Democrats — Mary Landrieu (Louisiana), Ben Nelson (Nebraska) and Mark Pryor (Arkansas) — voted with the Republicans to go ahead with the confirmation vote. Five Democrats and three Republicans did not vote. Bolton was eventually (1 August) appointed as a recess appointment by the President, thus avoiding the need for a vote in the Senate. This means Bolton can remain in his post until January 2007.

Who's who in American politics 2006

Executive branch

President	George W. Bush
Vice-President	Dick Cheney

The cabinet

Secretary of State	Condoleezza Rice
Secretary of Defense	Donald Rumsfeld
Secretary of the Treasury	John Snow
Secretary of Agriculture	Michael Johanns
Secretary of the Interior	Gale Norton
Attorney General (Justice Department)	Alberto Gonzales
Secretary of Commerce	Carlos Gutierrez
Secretary of Labor	Elaine Chao
Secretary of Health and Human Services	Michael Leavitt
Secretary of Education	Margaret Spellings
Secretary of Housing and Urban Development	Alphonso Jackson
Secretary of Transportation	Norman Mineta
Secretary of Energy	Samuel Bodman
Secretary of Veterans' Affairs	Jim Nicholson
Secretary of Homeland Security	Michael Chertoff

Executive Office of the President personnel

White House Chief of Staff	Andrew Card
Director of Office of Management and Budget	Joshua Bolten
National Security Adviser	Stephen Hadley
Chairman of National Economic Council	Allan Hubbard
Assistant to the President for Legislative Affairs	Candida Perotti Wolff
Trade Representative	Rob Portman
Press Secretary	Scott McClellan

Other executive branch personnel

Director of Central Intelligence Agency (CIA)	Porter Goss
Director of Federal Bureau of Investigation (FBI)	Robert Mueller
Chairman of the Joint Chiefs of Staff (JCS)	General Peter Pace

Legislative branch

President Pro Tempore of the Senate	Ted Stevens (R – Alaska)
Senate Majority Leader	Bill Frist (R – Tennessee)
Senate Majority Whip	Mitch McConnell (R – Kentucky)
Senate Minority Leader	Harry Reid (D – Nevada)
Senate Minority Whip	Dick Durbin (D – Illinois)
Speaker of the House of Representatives	Dennis Hastert (R – Illinois)
House Majority Leader	Roy Blunt (R – Missouri) (acting)
House Majority Whip	Roy Blunt (R – Missouri)
House Minority Leader	Nancy Pelosi (D – California)
House Minority Whip	Steny Hoyer (D – Maryland)

Senate Standing Committee chairs

Agriculture, Nutrition and Forestry	Saxby Chambliss	Georgia
Appropriations	Thad Cochran	Mississippi
Armed Services	John Warner	Virginia
Banking, Housing and Urban Affairs	Richard Shelby	Alabama
Budget	Judd Gregg	New Hampshire
Commerce, Science and Transportation	Ted Stevens	Alaska
Energy and Natural Resources	Pete Domenici	New Mexico
Environment and Public Works	James Inhofe	Oklahoma
Finance	Charles Grassley	Iowa
Foreign Relations	Richard Lugar	Indiana
Health, Education, Labor and Pensions	Mike Enzi	Wyoming
Homeland Security and Governmental Affairs	Susan Collins	Maine
Judiciary	Arlen Specter	Pennsylvania
Rules and Administration	Trent Lott	Mississippi
Small Business and Entrepreneurship	Olympia Snowe	Maine
Veterans' Affairs	Larry Craig	Idaho

House Standing Committee chairs

Agriculture	Bob Goodlatte	Virginia
Appropriations	Jerry Lewis	California
Armed Services	Duncan Hunter	California
Budget	Jim Nussle	Iowa
Education and the Workforce	John Boehner	Ohio
Energy and Commerce	Joe Barton	Texas
Financial Services	Michael Oxley	Ohio
Government Reform	Tom Davis	Virginia

Homeland Security	Peter King	New York
House Administration	Bob Ney	Ohio
International Relations	Henry Hyde	Illinois
Judiciary	James Sensenbrenner	Wisconsin
Resources	Richard Pombo	California
Rules	David Dreier	California
Science	Sherwood Boehlert	New York
Small Business	Donald Manzullo	Illinois
Standards of Official Conduct	Doc Hastings	Washington
Transportation and Infrastructure	Don Young	Alaska
Veterans' Affairs	Steve Buyer	Indiana
Ways and Means	Bill Thomas	California

Judicial branch

		President who appointed	Year appointed
Chief Justice	John Roberts	George W. Bush	2005
Associate Justices	John Paul Stevens	Ford	1975
	Antonin Scalia	Reagan	1986
	Anthony Kennedy	Reagan	1987
	David Souter	Bush	1990
	Clarence Thomas	Bush	1991
	Ruth Bader Ginsburg	Clinton	1993
	Stephen Breyer	Clinton	1994
	Samuel Alito	George W. Bush	2006